THE DIAMOND LINE

Are You Ready to Climb Aboard?

RICHARD FENTON & ANDREA WALTZ

The Diamond Line

Copyright © 2015 by

Richard Fenton & Andrea Waltz

ISBN: 978-0-9774393-6-2

PLEASE NOTE:

Every attempt has been made to ensure the photos included in this book are in the public domain. If for any reason a photo has been included in error, please contact the publisher at: Info@GoForNo.com.

Published by

C⬤URAGECRAFTERS

We invite you to visit the authors at:
www.GoForNo.com

Celebrating the 125th Anniversary of
Dr. Russell Conwell's *Acres of Diamonds*

Published by the John Y. Huber Company
Philadelphia, PA 1890

This Book Dedicated to

Dr. Russell H. Conwell

Author of the original *Acres of Diamonds*
story on which this work of fiction is based,
and a man far ahead of his time in the
understanding of the principles of success.

And to...

YOU.

The hard-working, success-bound entrepreneur—hungry for all the best life has to offer—and willing to do what it takes to get it.

Which, of course, includes reading.

To quote our friend Andrew Carnegie— whom you'll get to know better in the following pages...

"A library outranks any other one thing a community can do to benefit its people. It is a never-failing spring in the desert."

◊

FOREWORD BY
ERIC WORRE

I have long believed there are two ways to share knowledge with people. The first is to push facts and information out at people. The second is to pull people in through the use of a story. In fact, experts claim that stories are 22 times more memorable than facts alone.

I have no reason to doubt the validity of this, and have always admired writers who can teach me a lesson through a story.

To this day, many of the books that have helped me in my personal growth journey have been delivered through stories. My list of favorites includes:

- *"The Richest Man in Babylon"* by George Clason
- *"The Greatest Salesman in the World"* by Og Mandino
- *"The Alchemist"* by Paulo Coelho
- *"Jonathan Livingston Seagull"* and *"Illusions"* by Richard Bach
- *"The Fountainhead"* and *"Atlas Shrugged"* by Ayn Rand
- Along with a number of others.

"The Diamond Line" by Richard Fenton & Andrea Waltz is destined to take its place on the short list of classics.

Richard and Andrea first came on my radar screen when I discovered their personal development masterpiece, *"Go for No!"* And when they approached me to write the foreword to this book, I did not hesitate to say yes.

The Diamond Line is a clever reimagining of the motivational classic, *Acres of Diamonds,* by Russell Conwell, first published as a book in 1890. In *The Diamond Line,* however, you will be taken back to an imaginary moment in time before the book was written, having the chance to meet some of the greatest icons in history, including PT Barnum, Andrew Carnegie,

Frederick Douglass, and several other interesting and enlightening characters.

I'm sure we've all thought about being able to go back in time and meet some of our heroes.

In *The Diamond Line* you get the chance to do exactly that!

Russell Conwell not only believed it was possible for any person to become rich—*he believed it was a person's duty to do so*. Furthermore, Conwell felt that each of us is standing in the middle of our *acres of diamonds*—that everything we need to achieve success and personal wealth is right beneath our feet—if only we are able to recognize it.

I, too, believe that success is—*and has always been*—within you.

And now, with *The Diamond Line,* another tool has been placed in your hands to help bring that success to the surface in your life.

-Eric Worre

Author of *Go Pro* and founder of
Network Marketing Pro

www.networkmarketingpro.com

◇

"You can journey to the ends of the Earth in search of success, but if you're lucky, you will discover happiness in your own backyard."

–Russell H. Conwell

Track One:

iGSBE

It was one week before the 2014 IGSBE Conference, and I wanted to go badly. My wife, however, was completely against it.

"I know, Christopher," Katie said. "But we don't have the money. And besides, I can't get the time off," Katie added, "and you said that if we were going to go to IGSBE, we'd go together."

The 16th Annual IGSBE Conference was being held in New York City—IGSBE being an abbreviation for the International Gathering of Small Business Entrepreneurs—and I felt that attending the event would be good for our business.

I remained silent.

"Once the business grows a bit, we can do all sorts of things," Katie continued, filling the conversational void created by my unwillingness to accept the reality of the situation.

"Are you going to say something?" Katie asked.

Again, I remained silent.

"Well, I'm going to bed," Katie said. "Don't stay up too late, and turn off the TV when you come."

Katie kissed me on the forehead and walked off.

"I'm sorry. You're right," I said. "Maybe next year, huh?" But Katie didn't hear me. She was already gone. There was definitely an apology in my future.

I grabbed the remote and started flipping through channels, landing on a biography about the life of Apple co-founder Steve Jobs.

"So, Steve, what is *the* key to success?" the interviewer on TV asked.

9

"*The key?* I'm not sure there's a singular key," Jobs responded, "but I'd say to not let the noise of other's opinions drown out your own inner voice and to have the courage to follow your heart and intuition."

I'm trying, Steve, I really am.

Katie was right, of course. There was no way she could get time off during the school year, and money had been extremely tight since I'd made the decision to quit my job to focus on building the home-based business we'd started a year earlier.

WWSD? I wondered.

Steve would create another cool product and put another dent in the world—*were he still alive, of course.*

I grabbed my iPad—typed in "*eBay acres of diamonds*"—and pressed enter. I was curious to see how the one-hundred dollar bid I'd put on an 1890, hardcover first edition of Russell Conwell's classic, *Acres of Diamonds*, was doing.

I scrolled down and saw the current bid: *$285.* I was out of the running. *Way out.* I closed the iPad and thought about heading off to bed, but decided to watch the end of the Steve Jobs biography first.

*   *   *

"I have an idea," I heard Katie say from the doorway.

"What idea?"

"Well, you could go alone."

"Go to IGSBE alone? This is a team business," I said. "Either we go, or neither of us goes."

"Okay, Christopher, if you say so," Katie said.

Even going alone would be expensive, especially the airfare and the price of a hotel room in New York.

"What if you took the train?" Katie said, making her way over to the sofa and opening my iPad. "Look at this," she said a moment later.

She turned the iPad so I could see it.

Right at the top of the page there was an advertisement that read:

Introducing:
The Diamond Line
Chicago to New York City
$99 round trip!

"An experience you'll never forget."

Katie shot me a look. "Ninety-nine dollars is really cheap, Chris. And, you know, if you were willing to stay at a less expensive hotel across the river over in New Jersey?"

"It's totally up to you," I said.

A few keystrokes later, I had purchased a round trip ticket on The Diamond Line.

◇

"Do not neglect the day of
small things, for little
beginnings have big endings."

—Florence Scovel Shinn

Track Two:

GETTING TO UNION STATION

Katie pulled our blue Toyota SUV to the curb at the Amtrak station near our home in Naperville, Illinois, about forty miles west of downtown Chicago.

"I can't believe I'm going to be away from you for an entire week," I said. This would be the longest Katie and I had spent away from each other in the five years we'd been married. "It feels weird."

"I've got three things for you," Katie said with a smile.

The first was a paper sack filled with sandwiches and snacks, enough food to get me all the way to New York without having to spend a cent.

The second was a wrapped gift about the size of a paperback book. I had a pretty good idea what it was.

The third was a stack of envelopes held together with a rubber band. "Only open one envelope per day, okay? And no cheating!" she said.

I leaned over and kissed her. "This is going to be the best investment we've ever made, I promise."

"Enjoy the trip and do your best, okay?" Katie said. "And don't wait until you get to New York to talk to people. You never know who you might meet on the train."

* * *

After several quick stops we arrived at Chicago's Union Station where I would switch trains.

Erected on the west side of the Chicago River, Union Station was first built in 1881 and remodeled in 1925. The Beaux Arts great room, with its terracotta walls, marble floor brought in from Tennessee, and eighteen Corinthian columns soaring upward to the one-hundred-foot vaulted skylight ceiling, was truly awe-inspiring. Despite having lived in the Chicago area my entire life, this was my first time in the grand, historic building.

It took me a few minutes to understand how the station was organized—twenty-four tracks coming in from both the north and south—most of them underground, buried deep beneath city streets and skyscrapers.

I checked the travel board but was unable to find anything matching my ticket, so I made my way to the nearest information booth and found an elderly man dressed in a blue suit and bow tie. At least eighty-five years old, the man's skin was as wrinkled as his suit, which looked like it had never been pressed. He was alone behind the counter reading a newspaper.

"Excuse me," I said. "I'm passing through and—"

"No you're not," the man said without looking up.

"I'm sorry, what?"

"I said, no one passes through Union Station," the man repeated. "You can *connect* if you want to—meaning to get off one train and then get on another—but you can't *pass through*. The tricky part is getting on the right train. Pick the right platform, you get to where you're going. Pick the wrong platform, though, and who knows?"

The old man lifted his gaze and looked me over. "Let me guess," the man said. "You're looking for The Diamond Line."

"Yes, how did you know?" I asked, surprised.

"You have the look," the man said. Then he pointed a crooked finger and said, "The Diamond Line leaves from the far end of the station, that way. Walk all the way to the end. And when you think you've gone as far as you can go, and you want to turn around…"

"What?"

"Don't!" the man shouted. "Just keep going, going, going. Understand?"

"Yeah, I guess," I said.

"Don't guess," the man said, returning to his paper. "Just keep going."

It was clear that our conversation had reached its end.

I did as I was told, heading off in the direction the old man told me to go, and he was right.

It was a long, long way.

I walked for what seemed like forever—on and on, well past where the tracks ended—and just as I began to think I'd gone the wrong way I remembered what the old man had said:

> *"When you think you've gone as far as you can go, and you want to turn around, don't. Just keep going, going, going."*

So I kept going.

And then I saw it.

A small wooden sign that read:

The Diamond Line
≈ Boards Here Daily ≈

I set my bag down and took a look around. That's when I realized why Amtrak was offering such a great deal.

Apparently they had to.

I was the only one there.

◊

"Whatever you do, do it with all your might! Work at it, if necessary, early and late, in season and out of season, not leaving a stone unturned, and never deferring for a single hour that which can be done just as well now."

–P.T. Barnum

Track Three:

KATIES GIFT

I glanced at my watch for the third time, wondering when—*or if*—the train would arrive. I wished I'd brought a book to keep me occupied, and then remembered the gift Katie said she'd packed in my bag.

I unzipped my bag, found the gift, and unwrapped it.

It was a paperback version of the Russell Conwell classic *Acres of Diamonds*. I had seen an 1890 hardcover first edition of the book being auctioned on eBay several weeks earlier. The auction still had several days to go, but the price was already way beyond our budget.

I opened the paperback. On the inside front cover, Katie had written:

> *Christopher— I planned to give you this on your birthday, but thought you might enjoy having something to read on the train. I know it's not the first edition you really wanted, but I hope you like it anyway. –All my love… Katie.*

Suddenly I heard a voice call out, *"All aboard!"*

I looked up to see a train sitting on the tracks right in front of me. Apparently I'd been so engrossed in Katie's gift I hadn't even heard it arrive.

And the train was moving!

I grabbed my bag and raced after it, jumping on the metal steps just in time. I entered the railcar, still out of breath, and could see I would have no problem finding a place to sit.

I was the only person on the train.

I picked a spot to sit and settled in. And with nothing else to occupy my attention, I returned my attention to *Acres of Diamonds* and began reading...

> *When going down the Tigris and Euphrates rivers many years ago with a party of English travelers I found myself under the direction of an old Arab guide whom we hired up at Bagdad, and I have often thought how that guide resembled our barbers in certain mental characteristics. He thought that it was not only his duty to guide us down those rivers, and do what he was paid for doing, but also to entertain us with stories curious and weird, ancient and modern, strange and familiar. Many of them I have forgotten, and I am glad I have, but there is one I shall never forget.*
>
> *The old guide was leading my camel by its halter along the banks of those ancient rivers, and he told me story after story until I grew weary of his story-telling and ceased to listen. I have never been irritated with that guide when he lost his temper as I ceased listening. But I remember that he took off his Turkish cap and swung it in a circle to get my attention. I could see it through the corner of my eye, but I determined not to look straight at him for fear he would tell another story. But I did finally look, and as soon as I did he went right into another story.*
>
> *Said he, "I will tell you a story now which I reserve for my particular friends"... and when he emphasized the words "particular friends," I listened... and I have ever been glad I did!*

I felt my eyes getting tired and lowered the book. But when I did, I was shocked to see I was no longer alone. In fact, the passenger car was entirely packed with people! Had the train made a stop and picked up more people? Had I been so engrossed in the book I hadn't noticed?

I reached to turn down the corner of the page to mark my place, but before I could, a hand grabbed mine. I looked up to see it was the conductor, looking down on me like a stern father.

"Use this," the conductor snarled, handing me a purple satin bookmark. "One never folds the corners of a page, not of a true classic, and certainly not in a civilized society."

"It's just a paperback," I said.

"Oh, it is, is it?" the conductor said. Then, without waiting for a reply, the conductor continued up the aisle, asking each passenger for their ticket as he went along.

Oddly, he never asked for mine.

I placed the bookmark in my copy of *Acres of Diamonds*, then pulled out my cell phone to call Katie—only to discover there was no reception.

I would have to call her later.

I closed my eyes, the bright afternoon sun flashing through the windows of the railcar like a hypnotic strobe light. Before long, I drifted off to sleep, the paperback copy of Russell Conwell's *Acres of Diamonds* sitting in my lap.

◇

"As I grow older, I pay less attention to what men say. I just watch what they do."

—Andrew Carnegie

Track Four:

WAKING IN ANOTHER TIME

I t seemed like only moments had passed when the *Acres of Diamonds* book fell from my lap and hit my foot, waking me.

When I reached down to retrieve the book, I immediately noticed the scuffed gray linoleum floor had been replaced with highly polished wood.

I could also tell it was nighttime. *Could I have slept the entire day?*

I sat up slowly and looked around. *What in the...?*

It wasn't just the floor that had changed. *Everything was different.* The train car was old, like something out of a movie from the turn of the last century—yet it looked brand new. Shiny brass fittings and polished oak gleamed spotlessly, as if the train had just come off the factory assembly line or undergone a restoration by the Smithsonian.

I turned to look at the man seated on my left and found myself doing a double-take when I saw the Bowler hat on his head and giant handle-bar mustache on his face. He was someone straight out of a haberdasher's catalogue circa 1880 in a sharply tailored brown suit with narrow lapels, a starched wingtip-collared shirt, and a four-in-hand tie.

Across the aisle, another man sat reading a newspaper and smoking an enormous pipe. By the man's side sat two young girls, identically dressed in light blue dresses, trimmed in white lace at the collar and sleeves. Blue and white bonnets sat perched on the girl's heads, reminding me of some long-ago-forgotten butter ad.

As I glanced around, I saw that every person on the train was dressed in a similar manner.

"Excuse me," I said to the man across from me with the identically dressed girls.

The man lowered his paper. "Might you be speaking to me?"

It suddenly dawned on me I had no idea what I wanted to ask.

"Daddy, why is that man dressed so funny?" one of the two young girls asked. She was right, of course. I was the one who looked out of place, having dressed casually for the trip—in running shorts, Nike shoes, and a New York Yankees baseball cap.

The man slowly looked me over from head to toe, his eyes finally resting on my hat. "A fan of the Knickerbockers, I see," the man said.

"The Knickerbockers?" I repeated.

"Oldest baseball club in the league. Do you believe their future is bright?"

"Daddy, why is he in his undergarments?" one of the girls asked, her voice loud enough that virtually every head in the train car turned in our direction.

"Be polite, Sylvia," said the girl's father. "I am certain the young man has his reasons. "It is clear he is heading home to New York, and that is all we need know."

"Actually, I'm from Chicago," I said.

"Chicago?" the man bellowed. "Why in heaven's name would you live in one city, yet cheer for a ball club from another?" The entire railcar erupted in laughter at the man's comment, which seemed quite humorous to everyone but me.

I needed to be rescued. And I was.

"I, myself, am from the city of Philadelphia, yet I prefer the Boston Red Stockings club," came a voice, the laughter suddenly dying down. "Come sit with me, young man, and we shall discuss our teams."

* * *

I stood and walked back to where the man was sitting and lowered myself into an empty seat opposite him.

"I hope you don't mind my intrusion into your conversation," the man said, "but it appeared as if you needed someone to toss you a rope."

"That obvious, huh?" I said.

"Further, may I assume that you do not wish to discuss the game of baseball any more than I?"

"Right again," I said in agreement. "Baseball is the last thing on my mind right now."

"Is there a story you find yourself wishing to share?"

I wasn't really sure if explaining my situation was such a good idea. I had no desire to be placed in a straightjacket and locked up in some asylum somewhere, but I decided to take a chance. "Well, I'm not sure what's happening, or how I got here," I said.

"Did you board the wrong train?" the man asked.

"I'm afraid if I told you, you wouldn't believe me," I said.

"Well, then, if that be the case let us simply sit in the presence of each other's company and enjoy the sound of the train wheels on the metal rails below us as they deliver us to our destinations," the man said with a contented smile.

For the next five minutes, the man and I sat together— neither of us saying a word—as my mind raced through a variety of possibilities, none of which made any sense. Then I had a thought.

"What year is it?" I asked, breaking the silence.

"The year? Why, this is the year of our lord, eighteen-hundred and eighty-eight," the man said matter-of-factly. "Pray tell, what year did you assume it to be?"

I felt sick and leaned back in my seat and closed my eyes.

"You look ashen," the man said. "Perhaps I should call for some assistance?"

"No, no, just give me a second," I said, taking deep breaths and trying to calm myself down. "I'll be fine..."

I was wrong.

◊

"The game of life is a game of boomerangs. Our thoughts, deeds and words return to us sooner or later with astounding accuracy."

—Florence Scovel Shinn

Track Five:

MEETING RUSSELL CONWELL

When I awoke I found myself on a gurney in the train's hospital car, a doctor in a white coat standing over me. The doctor took his fingers and squeezed my neck.

"Doesn't appear to have mumps, and no sign of measles," the doctor said to the well-dressed man standing next to him. "In my opinion, the boy is simply overtired and perhaps dehydrated. I should think he is in no danger, but it would be best if someone were to watch over him in case of a relapse."

"You can release him in my care," my new friend said. "Is there something you wish to have me sign?"

"What is your name, son?" the doctor asked.

"Christopher, Christopher Powers," I replied.

The doctor wrote my name on a form and handed it to my new guardian, who signed his name as I attempted to pull myself together.

"There is the small matter of two dollars owed," the doctor said. "Do you wish to settle in cash, or would you prefer to have the balance billed to your account?"

"My account would be preferable," my new friend said.

"Very well. Let me just be sure I can read your signature," the doctor said, pulling his reading glasses from the pocket of his white coat. "Mr. Russell H. Conwell, is that correct?"

I felt a sudden tightness in my chest. *Did he just say...?*

"Yes," my new friend said, "but like you, I am a doctor—*Dr. Russell H. Conwell.*"

My gasp must have been audible.

Both men turned and looked at me, and—for the second time in less than an hour—the room went black around me.

◇ Dr. Russell H. Conwell ◇
1843-1925

Track Six:

"I HAVE WRITTEN NO SUCH BOOK"

Once I'd recovered and we'd returned to our seats in the passenger car, I said, "You asked me earlier what year I thought it was. Well, the answer to your question is 2014."

"Gad! More than one-hundred years from now?" Dr. Conwell asked.

I nodded.

Silence hung in the air.

"And there's more," I continued. "I was given a copy of your book today as a gift from my wife, something to read on the train."

"And what book might that be?" Dr. Conwell asked.

"Acres of Diamonds," I said.

"Acres of Diamonds?" Dr. Conwell repeated. "I have written no such book."

"Of course you have," I said. *"Acres of Diamonds* is the book you're famous for."

"That is simply an untruth," Conwell said, shaking his head from side to side. "Do you not think I would know it if—"

"Then how do you explain this?" I said, cutting him off and holding up the paperback.

"Let me see that!" he snapped, snatching the book from my hand and flipping through the first few pages. "Dear God, this is my diamond story."

"That's what I've been trying to tell you, Dr. Conwell."

"But where did this title come from?" he said, his face reddening with anger.

28

"Are you saying you didn't come up with the title *Acres of Diamonds?*" I asked.

"Come up with it? I've never even thought it!" Conwell snapped. "Not that it's a bad title, mind you—but it is not a title of my creation. I have told the diamond story many times, but never by this name."

"What title have you been using?"

"The Arab's Tale," Dr. Conwell said. "Now, I demand that you explain this parlor trick of yours."

Then it hit me. I grabbed the book from Dr. Conwell's hand and turned to the biography page. "Yes! That explains it."

"Explains what?"

"You said this is 1888, right? Well, it says here *Acres of Diamonds* was first published by the John Huber Company in 1890," I said. "The reason you don't know anything about writing it is because you haven't written it yet—*and won't for another two years.*"

"I know nothing of a John Huber or his company," Conwell said. "I have not a single clue as to who they are."

"Well, you will," I said.

Conwell remained silent for several seconds, then asked in a more friendly tone, "And this book—this *Acres of Diamonds*—does it do well?"

"Do well? It becomes an international bestseller. Between the book and the speech, you earn enough money to build Temple University. So, yeah, I'd say it does okay," I said with a bit of joking sarcasm in my voice.

"You mean Temple College?" he said.

"I'm guessing the name gets changed to University," I said. "In any case, you're the one who gets it built."

"Are you quite certain?" Conwell asked.

"Absolutely," I said.

◇

"People who are unable to motivate themselves must be content with mediocrity, no matter how impressive their other talents."

—Andrew Carnegie

Track Seven:

HATTIE MAY

Night fell, then morning came. But nothing had changed. I found myself still on the train in the year 1888 with Dr. Russell H. Conwell—author of one of the greatest motivational books of all time—and neither of us had the slightest explanation as to what was happening or why.

"Would it be fair to assume that book of yours has information regarding my eventual demise?" Dr. Conwell asked as we sat in the dining car having breakfast.

"This book of *yours*," I said. "And to answer your question, yes; there is a full biography at the back, including the date of..." I allowed my words to trail off, finding it impossible to say the word aloud.

"...my death," Dr. Conwell finished.

"Yes."

"I admit, every part of my being wishes to read what is written there, but I am quite certain the date of my demise is information which should be known only to God," Conwell said. "As such, it must remain unknown to me."

"Of course," I said, feeling somewhat uncomfortable that I knew the date Dr. Conwell was working so hard to avoid knowing—a date that was still thirty-seven years off.

"However..."

"However, what?" I asked.

"Without your referencing anything written in my biography, might you be willing to read me some of the story from that book?" Conwell asked.

"I don't think that would hurt anything," I said. I pulled the book from my bag and turned to the first page of the text, then began reading aloud:

When going down the Tigris and Euphrates rivers many years ago with a party of English travelers, making a circuit of the earth as the correspondent of the New York Tribune... *I found myself under the direction of an old Arab guide whom we hired up at Bagdad, and I have often thought how that guide resembled our barbers in certain mental characteristics.*

"My heavens!" Conwell exclaimed. "It is exactly as I tell it!"

"Of course it is because you wrote it," I said. "Well, you will write it."

"Amazing."

"Do you want me to continue?"

"Better yet, allow me to tell the next part as you read silently along and verify my accuracy," Conwell said, closing his eyes as if searching for a script written in the confines of his mind. Then he began...

He thought that it was not only his duty to guide us down those rivers, and do what he was paid for doing, but also to entertain us with stories curious and weird, ancient and modern, strange and familiar. Many of them I have forgotten, and I am glad I have, but there is one I shall never forget.

Dr. Conwell opened his eyes. "Well?"

"It's the same," I said. "Literally, word for word."

Dr. Conwell looked out the window of the train car. Then he turned back and said, "Do you know why I am here on this train?"

"How could I?" I said. "I don't even know why I'm here."

"I am on my return from Chicago, from attending the Republican National Convention to nominate a candidate for the office of president."

"Are you running for office?" I asked.

"Oh, heavens no!" Conwell said with a laugh. "I attended for the express purpose of meeting powerful men—more accurately, men with enough money to help fund a new church in my home city of Philadelphia. Our current structure is bursting at the seams, with members of the congregation standing in the hallways and out in the yard listening to sermons through opened windows."

"How much money do you need?" I asked.

"I am neither a builder nor architect, but I am told the amount needed is $109,000, perhaps more. To make matters worse," Conwell continued, "this amount is something I have publically promised to raise but have, as of yet, been unable to secure."

"Can't you just back out on the deal?" I asked.

"Perhaps," he said, "but doing so would result in the loss of our deposit."

"How much are we talking about?"

"Fifty-seven cents," Conwell said.

I couldn't help but laugh, thinking Dr. Conwell was making a joke. But then I could see how solemn and serious he was.

"It is not the amount," Conwell said. "It is where the fifty-seven cents came from that makes all the difference."

"Why? I'd love to hear the story," I said.

"It was during a Sunday morning service, and like all Sunday services of late, the church was packed to the gills. And this situation was especially true of the Sunday school room occupied by the children. And it was as I walked from one building to the next that I came upon a crying child. The child's name was Hattie May Waitt."

"What was she crying about?"

"Hattie May was distraught at not being allowed into the church that morning," Conwell continued. "But what option did we have? There was not enough room for another soul! So, I did the only thing I could think to do—I hoisted the small weeping child on my shoulders and carried her through the waiting crowds and into the church. It was because of this, unbeknownst to me, that little Hattie May decided that she would take it upon herself to raise money to expand the church, so that no other little boy or girl would have to be excluded from a service the way she had been."

"Wow," I said. "That's really something."

"Yes, it was quite something for a child to do on her own, but the story does not end there. I had no idea until a month later when Hattie May's parents came into my office carrying a small piggy bank and told me..."

Conwell stopped as if trying to hold back tears.

"Told you what?" I asked.

"Hattie May had contracted diphtheria, and passed away," Conwell said. "But not before she'd gone to collect money from everyone she knew—money that she intended to donate to the church—held in that small ceramic bank."

"Fifty-seven cents?" I asked, though I already knew the answer.

"Yes," Conwell said with tears welling in his eyes. "And that is why I am here. You see, I decided if that small, sweet child could take it upon herself to raise the first fifty-seven cents for a new church, then—by God—most certainly I could manage to raise the rest."

◇

"Many a man acquires a fortune by doing his business thoroughly, while his neighbor remains poor for life, because he only half does it. Ambition, energy, industry, perseverance, are indispensable requisites for success in business. Fortune always favors the brave, and never helps a man who does not help himself."

–P.T. Barnum

<u>Track Eight:</u>

FT. WAYNE, INDIANA

Russell Conwell had just finished telling the story about Hattie May and the fifty-seven cents when the door to the dining car opened and the conductor entered.

"Next stop, Ft. Wayne, Indiana," the Conductor called out, "Next stop, Ft. Wayne!"

"How long will the train be at the station?" Conwell asked the conductor as he strode down the aisle. The uniformed man checked his pocket watch and said, "The train will depart the station in exactly eighty-two minutes."

Conwell jumped to his feet with the enthusiasm of a much younger man and said, "Dress yourself in suitable clothing, Christopher, and be quick about it. I believe that if we leave this instant we will have just enough time."

*   *   *

Fifteen minutes later, after throwing on the only suit and tie I brought with me, I found myself trying to keep up with Dr. Conwell. I was in awe of my surroundings.

"Where are we going?" I asked as we made our way down a cobblestone street past well-dressed men on their way to work, newspaper boys shouting about the day's headline, and dodging the occasional horse-drawn carriage.

"Ah! This is perfect!" exclaimed Dr. Conwell when he spied a red-and-white-striped barbershop pole. We entered the shop and found it packed with men, reading their morning papers and patiently waiting for their turn in the chair.

Wasting no time, Russell Conwell made his way to the center of the room and bellowed, "Gentlemen, allow me to tell you a tale—a tale which I believe will leave you enriched far beyond the few pennies I will ask of you at the story's conclusion!"

I watched in amazement as everyone lowered their papers and listened as Dr. Russell Conwell told the *Acres of Diamonds* story...

The old guide was leading my camel by its halter along the banks of those ancient rivers, and he told me story after story until I grew weary of his story-telling and ceased to listen. But I remember that he took off his Turkish cap and swung it in a circle to get my attention. I could see it through the corner of my eye, but I determined not to look straight at him for fear he would tell another story. But I did finally look, and as soon as I did he went right into another story.

The old guide told me that there once lived not far from the River Indus an ancient Persian by the name of Ali Hafed. He said that Ali Hafed owned a very large farm, that he had orchards, grain-fields, and gardens; that he had money at interest, and was a wealthy and contented man. He was contented because he was wealthy... and wealthy because he was contented!

One day there visited that old Persian farmer one of these ancient Buddhist priests, one of the wise men of the East. He sat down by the fire and told the old farmer how this world of ours was made. He said that this world was once a mere bank of fog, and that the Almighty thrust His finger into this bank of fog, and began slowly to move His finger around, increasing the speed until at last He whirled this bank of fog into a solid ball of fire. Then it went rolling through the universe, burning its way through other banks of fog, and condensed the moisture without, until it fell in floods of rain upon its hot surface, and cooled the outward crust. Then the internal fires bursting outward through the crust threw up the mountains and hills, the valleys, the plains and prairies of this wonderful world of ours. If this internal molten mass came bursting out and cooled very quickly it became granite; less quickly copper, less quickly silver, less quickly gold, and, after

37

gold, diamonds were made. Said the old priest: "A diamond is a congealed drop of sunlight!"

Dr. Conwell paused then and strode around the room, making eye contact with each and every person there. After he was certain he had each man's undivided attention, he continued:

This is a scientific truth! A diamond is an actual deposit of carbon from the sun! The old priest told Ali Hafed that if he had one diamond the size of his thumb he could purchase the county, and if he had a mine of diamonds he could place his children upon thrones through the influence of their great wealth. And he said another thing I would never forget.

He declared that a diamond is the highest of God's mineral creations, as a woman is the highest of God's animal creations. I suppose that is the reason why the two have such a liking for each other!

The room erupted with laughter. It was clear that Dr. Russell Conwell knew how to work a room.

Ali Hafed heard all about diamonds, how much they were worth, and went to his bed that night a poor man. He had not lost anything, but he was poor because he was discontented, and discontented because he feared he was poor. He said: "I want a mine of diamonds!" And he lay awake all night.

Early in the morning he sought out the priest. I know by experience that a priest is very cross when awakened early in the morning, and when he shook that old priest out of his dreams, Ali Hafed said to him: "Will you tell me where I can find diamonds?"

Well, then, go along and find them. That is all you have to do—go and find them, and then you have them! 'But I don't know where to go.' 'Well, if you will find a river that runs through white sands, between high mountains, in those white sands you will always find diamonds.' 'I don't believe there is any such river.' 'Oh yes, there are plenty of them. All you have to do is to go and find them, and then you have them.' Said Ali Hafed: "I will go!"

So he sold his farm, collected his money, left his family in charge of a neighbor, and away he went in search of diamonds. He began his search, very properly to my mind, at the Mountains of the Moon. Afterward he came around into Palestine, then wandered on into Europe, and at last when his money was all spent and he was in rags, wretchedness, and poverty, he stood on the shore of that bay at Barcelona, in Spain, when a great tidal wave came rolling in between the pillars of Hercules, and the poor, afflicted, suffering, dying man could not resist the awful temptation to cast himself into that incoming tide, and he sank beneath its foaming crest, never to rise in this life again.

Conwell paused again, waiting for the wave of anger and frustration that was about to come:

"That is the worst story I have ever heard!" one of the barbershop patrons declared. "You wish to receive payment for such morbidity?" another asked. "What kind of motivation is it to learn that the hero is not only killed, but has thrown himself into the sea due to his own failure?" a third man demanded.

"Ah, but that's the thing!" Conwell said with a gleam in his eye. "This is but the first chapter of the story! But, fear not, for I am about to write a book that will chronicle every detail of this tale, including an ending that will leave you stunned in amazement!"

"I believe I would buy such a book," one man said.

"As would I," declared another.

"Very well, then," Conwell said, pulling a stack of envelopes from his jacket pocket and passing them out. "If you will write your name and address on one of these envelopes—and place a mere two dollars inside—I shall mail a copy to you upon its publication."

I stood and watched in wonder as virtually every man in the room dug into their pockets and placed their envelopes in Dr. Conwell's outstretched hand.

"This book of yours, Conwell," a man called out. "What is it titled?"

Dr. Conwell turned and looked in my direction, smiled, and said, "It shall be called *Acres of Diamonds*!"

◊

"Without struggle, there can be no progress. Those who profess to favor freedom, and yet depreciate agitation, are men who want crops without plowing up the ground."

–Frederick Douglass

Track Nine:

TELL ME ABOUT YOURSELF

We re-boarded the train in the nick of time and ate lunch together in the dining car.

"Do you wish to make another visit with the doctor?" Dr. Conwell asked.

"No," I said. "Unless they've got a psychiatrist on board, I don't think there is anything they can do to help me."

Conwell laughed. "So, Christopher, tell me about yourself. Are you married?"

"Yes," I said. "Her name is Katie. We've been married for five years now."

"And have you and Katie been blessed with children?"

"Not yet," I said. "We're planning to when the time is right."

"Trust me, Christopher—the time is never right for children," Dr. Conwell said. "You just decide, move ahead, and have them."

"What about you?" I asked. "I'm embarrassed to say I know nothing about you."

"Except for the date I go to meet my maker," Conwell said.

I wished I didn't. "It's like carrying an enormous weight," I said.

"Imagine how God must feel," Conwell said.

"So, have you ever been married?" I asked, not realizing the chord I was about to strike.

"Twice," Conwell replied. "My first wife left this Earth in 1872, leaving me with two small children."

"I'm sorry," I said.

42

"No need to be sorry, Christopher," Conwell said. "I believe God has a plan, even if we do not know what that plan is at the time—like you—being here on this train. There is certainly a reason for it, though we are not privy to precisely why at this time."

I hoped he was right.

"When my wife died, I asked God why he had taken her, and do you know how he answered?"

I shook my head, no.

"He answered with the gift of a third child—a girl, by my second wife—who would never have been born without each event in my life having happened exactly as it had," Conwell said with conviction. "But enough about me. Tell me, Christopher, how do you and Katie make your living in the year 2014?"

"Well, Katie's a third grade school teacher, and I'm in the process of getting our network marketing business off the ground."

"What is this endeavor of which you speak? It sounds rather complicated," Conwell said.

Again, I realized how different everything was 125 years earlier. The concept of network marketing didn't even exist. So, how to explain it?

"You know how salespeople are the backbone of any business, right?" I asked.

"Certainly," Conwell said. "I have read the number is rapidly approaching one-hundred thousand."

"We've got that many people in just one leg of our company."

"One leg?" Conwell said.

This was going to be more difficult than I thought.

"The main point is network marketing companies offer products through a network of people who don't really work for the company," I said. "They work for themselves."

"Entrepreneurial spirits, are they?" Conwell asked.

"Yes, that's the perfect term for it," I said. "And each person is responsible for finding other entrepreneurial spirits to join them, which is why I was headed to New York."

"There aren't enough of these entrepreneurial spirits available in Chicago?"

"No, of course there are," I said.

"Have you read my *Acres of Diamonds* book cover to cover?" Conwell asked.

"Not yet," I said. "I'd just started it when I boarded the train."

"Interesting," Conwell said. "Perhaps I know why you are on the train after all."

"Really? Why?"

"Well, let us allow things to play themselves out a bit and—if I am right—I shall share my theory with you," Conwell said.

"Okay," I said.

"For now, may I ask your advice on something?"

"Sure," I said, finding it impossible to imagine anything I was qualified to offer advice on.

"A good friend of mine—Asa Candler, an entrepreneurial spirit much like yourself—is launching his own enterprise. For years, Asa made his living as a lowly peddler hawking John Pemberton's syrup to restaurants. However, through hard work, Asa has earned enough to buy Pemberton's formula for the sum of $2,300, an outrageous price for a simple formula, do you not think?"

"I don't know," I said. "What's the syrup called?"

"Pemberton called his drink Coca-Cola," Conwell said. "My friend, however, is thinking of changing the name."

I almost choked. "I think your friend made a good decision in buying the formula," I said.

"That is good to hear," Conwell said. "And what of the name?"

"Tell him to stick with Coca-Cola."

◇

"There is not a poor person in the United States who was not made poor by his own shortcomings. It is all wrong to be poor."

–Russell H. Conwell

MEETING FLORENCE

I tried several times to reach Katie, but it became obvious my cell phone was useless—it being the year 1888 and all. So I did what I always did when things seemed outside my control.

I took a nap.

When I woke up an hour later, I discovered a girl, who looked to be sixteen or seventeen years of age, checking me out. She had long black hair down to her shoulders, big dark eyes, and cheekbones that were so pronounced she almost looked malnourished. What made her stand out most, however, was that she was the only person on the train not wearing a hat.

"Can I help you?" I asked.

"I heard you speaking with Dr. Conwell," the girl said.

"Do you know Dr. Conwell?" I asked.

"Not personally," she said, "but I have heard him speak several times. Dr. Conwell is a great man."

"I agree," I said. "Are you alone here on the train?"

"Yes," she said. "I am on my way back home after several days spent in Chicago to further my art studies, but I also intend to be an author and lecturer like Dr. Conwell."

That explained why she was looking at me. She wanted to meet Dr. Conwell. "I could introduce you if..."

"That would be appreciated, but it is actually you I desire to speak with."

That caught me off guard, "Me? Why?"

"Because you know things about the future," she said.

47

"So, you've been eavesdropping?" I said with a tinge of annoyance in my voice.

"It is not as if you have been at all discreet," the girl said. "You could not have stood out more if you were dressed in a gorilla costume and wearing ballerina slippers."

"Oh?" I replied, finding myself defensive, even though the girl was totally right. "Well, you stand out yourself, you know."

"Me? I stand out?" she said. "How so, exactly?"

"You aren't wearing a hat," I said.

"That's your best retort?" the girl asked. "That I am hatless?"

I couldn't have felt more stupid if I tried.

"Let me enlighten you as to why I am without a hat," the girl continued. "I do not wear a hat because I do not like hats and refuse to be a slave to fashion, engaged in the pitiful behavior of following others in pursuit of acceptance by donning the current fads."

There was something about the girl—poise, confidence, guts, perhaps all of the above—that caused me to like her immediately.

Besides, I needed all the friends I could get.

"What's your name?" I asked.

The girl rose to her feet before responding. "My name is Florence Scovel from the fine city of Philadelphia."

I stood and held out my hand. "My name is…"

"…Christopher, of Chicago, Illinois," Florence said, taking my hand and shaking it firmly. "May I?"

Florence lowered herself on the wooden seat next to me and wasted no time getting to the point. "Now, Christopher of Chicago—without the waste of additional time—please tell me everything you know regarding the future."

48

◊ Florence Scovel Shinn ◊
1871-1940

Track Eleven:

TELLING OF THE FUTURE

A s was the case with Dr. Conwell, I was pretty sure that telling Florence about the future was a breach of universal etiquette, and I'd seen enough time-travel movies to know it was a bad idea to screw around with the space-time continuum.

Florence had other thoughts on the subject.

"Any agreements you have with Dr. Conwell are strictly between you and he," Florence said.

"And the consequences be damned?" I asked.

"Yes," Florence said. "There are consequences to all actions, and might I remind you there will be consequences to your *not* telling me what you know."

She had a point. Besides, there was no use fighting it— Florence Scovel was a force of nature not to be denied. "So what do you want to know?"

"I wish to know what the future is like, and how things have changed. Are people more comfortable? What wonderful inventions have been created? I want to know it all!"

"You got a hundred years to spare?" I said.

"Excellent point," Florence said. "How about we start with the biggest event between this moment and your time."

"I guess the biggest thing that happens is in 1969, when the United States lands a man on the moon."

"That is not possible!" Florence shrieked, causing everyone in the train car to turn and look at us. I realized my mistake instantly. If I were to share information about the future, I would have to take it a little slower.

"Maybe we should do this chronologically, starting today and working forward," I said.

50

"Perhaps that would be best," Florence said, having calmed down.

Thinking that fifteen years in the future wouldn't be too much of a leap for Florence, I started again. "In 1903, Orville and Wilber Wright complete the first successful airplane flight."

I was wrong.

"Dear God!" Florence shouted, every head turning once again in our direction. Florence lowered her voice. "Are you telling me that man will take flight in a mere fifteen years' time?"

"They only get off the ground for a few seconds, but yes—and it changes the world," I said quietly. "People who'd never traveled more than a few hundred miles in their lives start going all over the world."

"My, what I would give to witness such an event!" Florence said. "Tell me, Christopher, where does this historic moment take place?"

In for penny, in for a pound.

"It's a place called Kitty Hawk," I said. "In the Carolinas."

Florence's eyes were bright with excitement, as if she were glowing inside. "What else?" she asked. "Please, tell me more! What happens next?"

I found myself wishing I'd had a history book with me, or at a minimum having paid better attention in history class. "I guess the next thing is Henry Ford's invention of the assembly line. This makes it possible to build cars—automobiles—cheaply enough that anyone can own one. By the year 1950, people will be driving all across the country on a system called highways."

"Can this all be true?" Florence asked.

I nodded. "But there's some bad stuff, too, Florence. The Spanish flu is going to kill something like one-hundred million people in 1918 or thereabout. If I remember right, it mostly kills younger people, so you're going to want to watch out for that."

"You say this as if it is written in stone," Florence said. "Certainly there's a way to stop such a tragedy?"

"I don't think so," I said. "The good news is there are many advances in medicine—antibiotics and vaccines for polio and measles and smallpox—which saves millions of people who would have died."

"Beyond belief," she replied.

"Getting back to our chronology," I said, "the next big thing will be the stock market crash of 1929, followed by The Great Depression. But, as usual, America comes out of it okay by the end of World War I."

"The entire world is at war?"

"Yeah, and there's a second one against Germany again. But Japan gets involved by attacking Pearl Harbor. Then we invade France, take out Adolph Hitler, and then Albert Einstein figures out how to split the atom and then we—"

"Pearl Harbor?" Florence asked, trying desperately to keep up.

"It's in Hawaii."

"There's so much to take in," Florence said. "Please, Christopher, just tell me this. Is life better in the future?"

"Better? Better is a pretty subjective term," I said. "But, yeah—overall things are better for virtually everyone."

"That is good to hear," Florence said. "What of the other inventions to come?"

Again, I didn't want to jump too far ahead. "Well, we create a thing called television, which allows pictures to be transmitted through the air and people can watch shows on a box in your living room. Actually, if my cell phone worked we could watch TV right here on the train."

"I do not understand what you are saying," Florence said, looking dismayed. Of course she didn't understand. How could she?

"A cell phone is a telephone you carry with you wherever you go," I said, pulling out my cell and showing it to her. "I have no reception right now—probably because cell phone towers won't be invented for another hundred years—but the battery is still charged so at least the games work."

"Games? Such as chess and backgammon?" she asked.

"Yeah, but there are a lot of others, too, like Candy Crush and Angry Birds," I said. "Here, I'll show you."

I showed Angry Birds to her on the cell phone screen. "The point of the game is to fling different kinds of birds at the pigs, and try to kill them."

"Please tell me this is not the best of what the future brings?" Florence said. "Murdering pigs with frustrated fowl?"

"Angry birds," I corrected. "And, no, there's so much more—indoor plumbing, refrigerators, frozen food, laptops, electricity, washing machines, vacuum cleaners, microwave ovens, the Internet. Oh, and people finally come to the conclusion that smoking causes lung cancer," I said just a bit more loudly than necessary so that some of the many smokers in the train car could hear me through the haze of pipe and cigar smoke.

"Smoking kills people?" Florence asked.

"Absolutely, smoking is one of the worst things you can do," I said again, even more loudly this time.

"The future you describe, it sounds like a place of madness," Florence said.

"Yes, I guess it does," I said.

"Please do not misunderstand me, Christopher," Florence said. "It sounds like a place of wonderful, glorious madness! A place where there are no limits—whether you are a man or woman—and anything is possible. And to think there is talk about shutting down the patent office."

"Shut down the patent office?" I asked in disbelief. "Why would anyone want to shut down the patent office?"

"The commissioner, a man by the name of Charles Duell, has the notion that everything that can be invented already has been," Florence said with disgust. "I have always believed him to be a fool, and now—with your tales of the many fabulous inventions to come—you have confirmed it."

All this talk about inventions suddenly made me think of something. "Has Alexander Graham Bell invented the telephone already?" I asked.

"Yes, we've had telephones since I was a young girl. They are still very new, however, so not everyone has one yet like in your future."

"Do you think you could help me find one, Florence?"

"Certainly, but under one condition." Florence said.

"Yes, I'd be glad to introduce you to Dr. Conwell," I said.

"Actually," Florence said with a sly smile, "I was hoping you'd allow me to play Angry Birds."

◇

"If you want to be happy, set
a goal that commands your
thoughts, liberates your energy,
and inspires your hopes."

_Andrew Carnegie

Track Twelve:

CLEVELAND, OHIO

Next stop, Cleveland, Ohio!" the conductor announced, advising passengers who exited the train to re-board no later than 7:30 p.m.

I glanced at my watch and saw it was 5:42 p.m.

"If we leave right away," I said to Florence, "we should be able to find a phone and get back before the train departs."

"Ah, Christopher, there you are!" Dr. Conwell called out, working his way up the aisle of the passenger car toward us. "I thought Cleveland an excellent opportunity to share the *Acres of Diamonds* tale again. Would you care to come along?"

"Sure, but would it be okay if I brought a friend along?" I asked.

"And who might this friend be?" Conwell asked.

"Dr. Conwell, this is Florence Scovel," I said.

"Good evening, Dr. Conwell," Florence said, extending her hand. "I was present at your talk at the Baptist Temple in Philadelphia two years ago. Very eye-opening, if I may say so."

Conwell smiled and looked pleased. "It is a delight to meet you, Florence. I appreciate the kind words."

"Florence is going to help me find a telephone," I said. "It probably won't work, but I have to try and reach Katie."

"Then we best move along if we wish to accomplish our objectives," Conwell said.

* * *

Dr. Conwell led Florence and I down a long street through the center of Cleveland—past bakeries and butcher shops and live playhouses—until we came upon a firehouse.

"Ah, the perfect place to present my talk!" Dr. Conwell exclaimed.

"Do you think the fire station would have a phone?" I asked.

"I would think they should," Florence said.

"Perhaps, but I would think the police station a better bet," Conwell said. "Have you got money?"

Money? The answer to that was yes and no.

"Here," Conwell said, digging in the pocket of his trousers and pulling out several coins. "Making a telephonic call is not an inexpensive matter."

"Thank you. Florence and I will catch up to you as soon as we can," I said, checking my cell phone one last time—just in case—only to discover the battery was completely dead.

"Sorry," Florence said with a sheepish grin. "I hope I did not destroy it. I was playing with your Angry Birds, and it went dark and stopped."

"It's okay," I said. "The phone is the most important thing, and it hasn't worked since I got on The Diamond Line, and there's no reason to think it's going to start working now."

Unfortunately, finding a phone was harder than either of us thought. Finally, Florence spotted a police officer. "Could you direct us to your police station?" Florence asked.

The cop looked me up and down, checking out my odd clothing. "Is this man bothering you, miss?"

"Not in the least," Florence said. "We simply need to find a telephone. Is the station equipped with one?"

"We have a telephone," the cop said, my spirits lifting. "But the device has not been operational for several days. A wonderful invention when it operates. Might I suggest you try the hospital? It is about one mile from here in that direction."

The cop pointed his finger to the west, and ten minutes later Florence and I entered the lobby of Cleveland General.

* * *

The phone looked just like something out of an old movie—a wooden box mounted to the wall with a handset on top in a metal cradle—and two silver bells on one side, and a crank handle on the other.

"How do I dial it?" I asked.

"You have never used a phone?" Florence asked.

"Not one like this. This thing is as new to me as my cell phone is to you."

"You simply pick up the handset, and tell the operator the name of the party you wish to connect to," Florence said. I lifted the handset as Florence instructed and placed it to my ear, but nothing happened. "Oh, I forgot that you must crank it first."

Florence reached over and cranked the handle several times and—sure enough, a moment later—an operator came on the line. "Whom do you wish to ring?" the female operator said.

"The number I'm trying to reach is—"

"Name of the party, please," the operator said.

"Um, her name is Katie Powers, and—"

"What exchange is your party in?" the operator asked.

"Exchange? What's an exchange?" I said.

"Klondike? Spring? Butterfield?" the operator asked. "I must know the exchange."

"I don't know," I stammered. "Her name is Katie Pow—"

"I am sorry sir, but I cannot make your connection with the information provided. Thank you for using the Bell Telephone Company."

The line went dead.

I placed the handset back in its silver cradle, feeling totally defeated.

"I am truly sorry, Christopher," Florence said.

Just then, the bell on the side of the phone began to ring.

I knew the call couldn't possibly be for me, of course, but I reached out and lifted the handset anyway.

At first, all I could hear was a loud crackling sound, but then—to my immense shock and surprise—I heard Katie's voice.

It was very faint, as if it had traveled a million miles.

But it was her.

"Katie?" I said loudly. "Katie, is that you?"

"Christopher?" I heard her ask.

"Yes!" I practically yelled. "Yes, it's me!"

"You sound so far away," Katie said.

She had no idea.

"How did you know to call me here?" I asked.

"What do you mean?" Katie said. "You called me?"

This was getting creepier by the minute.

"Where are you?" she asked. "When you didn't call I got worried. Are you at the conference?"

"No," I said, shouting to make sure she could hear me over the crackling sound on the phone line. "I'm in Cleveland."

"Cleveland?" Katie said. "Why are you in Cleveland?"

"Something happened, Katie..."

"Are you in the hospital? Are you hurt?" she asked frantically.

"It's hard to explain, but I think it's got something to do with the book you bought me."

"*Acres of Diamonds*?" she asked. The crackling sound was so loud now I could barely make out what she was saying. *"Tell me where you are."*

"I'm on a train with Russell Conwell," I said.

There was a long silence, then Katie said, "That's not funny, Christopher. Tell me the truth. Where are you?"

But before I could respond, the cracking noise abruptly stopped and there was nothing but silence.

"Katie? Katie!" I yelled into the phone, but it was no use.

She was gone.

*   *   *

When Florence and I reunited with Dr. Conwell on the train, he was ecstatic. "They ate it up!" he said. "I received seventy-two dollars in orders. How I wish you could have been there."

"Things took longer than we thought," I said.

"Christopher talked to his wife across the expanse of time," Florence said.

"Is this true, Christopher?"

"Yes," I said. "I don't know how, but it was her. It was Katie."

"It was truly a miracle," Florence said.

"Perhaps," Dr. Conwell said. "That, or God has taken a position working for Mr. Bell."

◇

"Most people consider life a battle, but it is not a battle, it is a game."

–Florence Scovel-Shinn

Track Thirteen:

HARRISBURG, PENNSYLVANIA

"How did all these people know to be here?" I asked as the train pulled into the station in Harrisburg.

"I have no earthly idea," Conwell said, peering through the passenger car windows at the crowd gathered beneath a sea of black umbrellas in a steadily falling rain.

"Word of your talk must have spread," Florence said.

Dr. Conwell pulled himself away from the glass. "Would either of you like to join me? Perhaps say a few words?"

Sharing the platform with an icon like Russell Conwell would be a dream for some people, but my fear of public speaking—even if just a few words—made it impossible for me to accept the invitation.

"I think I'd like to experience the moment with the crowd," I said. "But thanks."

"I do not care what Christopher wants to do," Florence said. "I do have a few words I would like to share—from a woman's perspective."

*   *   *

Minutes later, I found myself in the crowd—shoulder-to-shoulder with five hundred men and women in a driving rain, working my way from umbrella to umbrella—each of whom had come to hear Dr. Conwell deliver his newly titled *Acres of Diamonds* talk.

Finally, the rear doors of the train swung open, and Dr. Conwell stepped out on the rear platform of the train to thunderous applause, with young Florence Scovel by his side.

Dr. Conwell remained silent, patiently waiting for the chants of *"Speech! Speech!"* to die away. Then he cleared his throat and began:

Thank you, dear friends, for braving the rain of this unusually cold and rainy day! It is my sincere promise that you shall consider the effort worthwhile. That said, I am astonished that so many people should care to hear this story, which is a study in psychology, one which breaks all rules of oratory and departs from the precepts of rhetoric.

I have sometimes studied for a year upon a lecture and made careful research, putting too much work on it, then presented the lecture just once—and never delivered it again! But this lecture, this had no work on it—thrown together perfectly at random, spoken offhand without any special preparation, told from time to time to friends at dinner, but never rising to the level of being a lecture, an entire failure.

Until now, until this very moment, where I have come to predict that this lecture—which I now call Acres of Diamonds—will become the most famous of all and will one day be found in books in nearly every library. Do not ask me how I know such things, but trust me when I tell you, I do.

The "Acres of Diamonds" about which I have mentioned are to be found in this city, in Harrisburg, or for that matter from wherever you may have traveled to be here. In fact, many have found them! And what any man has done, any other man can do.

And now I shall share the tale...

Dr. Conwell paused for a full ten seconds, allowing the excitement to build, and then launched into the story:

When going down the Tigris and Euphrates rivers many years ago with a party of English travelers...

Dr. Conwell delivered the portions of the story I'd heard him share already—about Ali Hafed selling his farm and setting about to find the diamonds, only to fail in his quest.

Just as the audience had in the barber shop in Ft. Wayne, the crowd gasped in horror when Conwell reached the point in the story when Ali Hafed flung himself into the sea.

Knowing how to work the crowd, Dr. Conwell waited for the precise right moment to jump back in. "But there is more!" he shouted.

When that old guide told me that awfully sad story, he stopped the camel I was riding on and went back to fix the baggage that was coming off another camel, and I had an opportunity to muse over his story while he was gone. There seemed to be no beginning, no middle, no end, nothing to it. That was the first story I had ever heard told in my life—and would be the first one I ever read—in which the hero was killed in the first chapter. I had but one chapter of that story, and the hero was dead!

The crowd nodded in agreement and relaxed, knowing there was more to come.

When the guide came back and took up the halter of my camel, he went right ahead with the story, into the second chapter, just as though there had been no break, saying: "One day, the man who purchased Ali Hafed's farm led his camel into the garden to drink. And as that camel put its nose into the shallow water of that garden brook, Ali Hafed's successor noticed a curious flash of light from the white sands of the stream. He pulled out a black stone with an eye of light reflecting all the hues of the rainbow. He took the pebble into the house and put it on the mantel that covered the central fires and forgot all about it.

A few days later, this same old priest came in to visit Ali Hafed's successor, and the moment he opened that drawing-room door he saw that flash of light on the mantel, and he rushed up to it, shouting, "Here is a diamond! Has Ali Hafed returned?"

"Oh no, Ali Hafed has not returned, and that is not a diamond. That is nothing but a stone we found right out here in our own garden."

"But," the priest replied, "I tell you I know a diamond when I see it, and I know positively that is a diamond."

Then together they rushed out into that old garden and stirred up the white sands with their fingers, and lo! There came up other more beautiful and valuable gems than the first. "Thus," the guide said to me—and, friends, it is historically true—"was discovered the diamond mine of Golconda, the most magnificent diamond mine in all the history of mankind, excelling the Kimberly itself. The Kohinoor and the Orloff of the crown jewels of England and Russia, the largest on earth, came from that mine."

When that old Arab guide told me the second chapter of his story, he then took off his Turkish cap and swung it around in the air again to get my attention to the moral. Those Arab guides have morals to their stories, although they are not always moral.

The guide swung his hat and he said to me, "Had Ali Hafed remained at home and dug in his own cellar, or underneath his own wheat-fields or in his own garden, instead of wretchedness, starvation, and death by suicide in a strange land, he would have had his acres of diamonds."

When he'd finished, the crowd went absolutely wild with applause. It was unlike anything I had ever witnessed.

The biggest surprise, however, was yet to come.

◇ Phineas Taylor (P.T.) Barnum ◇
1810-1891

Track Fourteen:

FLORENCE GETS HER CHANCE

Russell Conwell had just finished delivering his Acres of Diamonds talk to the enthusiastic crowd who'd gathered at the Harrisburg train station. But then he did something no one expected.

Conwell turned to the young girl who'd been standing on the platform with him and said, "Florence, would you care to share a few words to the gathering?"

Such an invitation would have thrown most people into a state of utter panic, but Florence seemed calm and in total control of herself. What an amazing showing of poise for someone so young. Where does such confidence come from? I wondered.

With an air of confidence I'm sure I could not have mustered, Florence stepped forward and began...

If there is one thing I have learned in my long and tumultuous seventeen years on this Earth...

The comment brought immediate laughter from the audience before she continued:

...It is that, while we cannot always control our thoughts, we can control our words. And it is the repetition of the right words that impresses the subconscious, and we are then the master of the situation.

In the sixth chapter of Jeremiah, we read: "I set a watchman over you, saying, Hearken to the sound of the trumpet."

Your success and happiness in life depend upon the watchman at the gate of your thoughts, which sooner or later, crystallizes on the external.

Sadly, people think by running away from a negative situation, they will be rid of it, but the same situation confronts them wherever they go.

Many people are cutting out fear pictures, seeing things that are not divinely planned. However, with the "single eye," man sees only the truth. He sees through evil, knowing that out of it comes good. He transmutes injustice into justice, and disarms his seeming enemy by sending out goodwill to all.

We read in mythology of the giant Cyclops, said to have inhabited Sicily. These giants had only one eye in the middle of the forehead.

Well, I say that you are indeed a giant when you have a single eye! Every thought will be a constructive thought, and every word, a word of power.

Let the third eye be the watchman at your gate! If, therefore, thine eye be single, thy whole body is full of light! With the single eye your body will be transformed into your spiritual body—the "body electric" made in God's likeness and image!

By seeing clearly the perfect plan, we can redeem the world with our inner eye, seeing a world of peace... and a world of plenty... and a world of love and goodwill toward one another!

I could not believe my eyes! Just as they had for Dr. Conwell, the crowd burst into wild applause.

Dr. Conwell stepped forward and hugged Florence, almost as if he were a proud father, and turned to address the crowd one last time:

In leaving, I say—that should you be thinking to yourself, "What does one so young know of life?" Then you shall not be cheating Florence; you shall be cheating yourself! For she is correct! We should enjoy a world filled with peace, love, and goodwill for one another, and I wish these things and more for each of you gathered here today.

68

But Florence also used another word, a word I hope you caught for its supreme importance—it was the word "plenty."

I say that you should enjoy a life of plenty, and let me not mince words—by plenty, I mean that you ought to get rich!

The crowd cheered and applauded.

What is more, I say you should not only get rich, I say it is your duty to get rich! How many of you, my pious brethren, are thinking now: "Does Dr. Conwell, a Christian minister, spend his time going up and down the country advising young people to get rich—to get money?" Yes, of course I do! People say, "Isn't that awful! Why don't you preach the gospel instead of preaching about man's making money?"

Because to make money by honest means is to preach the gospel! That is the reason!

To make money honestly is to live the way God wishes for us all! That is my gospel! That is the reason! What other reason does a man need?

Virtually every person began making their way toward the rear platform of the train with envelopes stuffed with cash.

*   *   *

An hour later we were back in the main railcar, heading east out of Harrisburg toward Allentown, Pennsylvania, and then New York City.

"You do realize what a miracle your being here is and how much I appreciate what you have done, do you not?" Dr. Conwell said.

"Me? I didn't do anything," I said.

"Oh, but you have Christopher. You are the answer to my prayers," Conwell declared. "You see, when I was unsuccessful in my endeavors at raising money in Chicago, I asked God to show me a way—to send a messenger—to tell me how to raise the money myself. Then I closed my eyes," Conwell said. "And when I opened them, there you were."

◊

"Begin where you are, and what you are."

–Russell H. Conwell

Track Fifteen:

MY ACRE OF DIAMONDS

As I sat in the dining car that afternoon, I found myself thinking less about the strange situation I'd found myself in, and more about the reason why.

Why had the universe placed me here?

I wolfed down a plate of beef stroganoff and washed it down with a big glass of ice-cold milk—courtesy of Dr. Conwell—who had arranged for me to charge my meals to his account since I had no spendable cash.

I opened my journal, something I had been doing for several years now, and summarized everything that had happened, starting with the moment I woke up on the train and found myself back in the year 1888. The more I wrote, the more I realized things boiled down to three inescapable conclusions:

Conclusion #1: *This wasn't a dream. I know what dreams feel like, and this was happening for real...*

Conclusion #2: *What was happening was connected to Katie's gift...*

Conclusion #3: *There must be a lesson I was supposed to learn from this—if not, why was this happening?*

I began to think about the main lesson conveyed in the *Acres of Diamonds* story, and Dr. Conwell's premise that every resource a person needs can be found right where they are.

And that's when it hit me:

I was the guy who was abandoning his acres of diamonds. The story was about me. I was Ali Hafed, gone off to find his diamond, when all along they were right there in my own backyard.

71

Prospecting for business...

Prospecting for people...

Prospecting for diamonds...

Prospecting for gold...

It was all the same thing!

I thought about my network marketing business and realized how much time and energy I'd wasted over the years looking out there somewhere for my *acre of diamonds*.

And the IGSBE Conference was a perfect example! *What was I expecting to find in New York that didn't exist at home? What resources were available a thousand miles away that were unavailable to me in Chicago?*

I shoved my journal back in my bag, eager to find Dr. Conwell and Florence and tell them about my breakthrough. And then, as important as this experience had been...

I wanted to get off this train...

I wanted to get back to Katie...

I wanted to get back to Chicago...

I wanted to get back to work!

◇

"Those who really desire to attain an independence, have only to set their minds upon it, and adopt the proper means, as they do in regard to any other object which they wish to accomplish, and the thing is easily done."

—P.T. Barnum

Track Sixteen:

THE WRINKLED OLD MAN

I stood to leave the dining car, but just as I did, a man slid into the seat on the opposite side of the table.

"So, you figured it out, did you?"

I couldn't believe my eyes. It was the wrinkled old man from the train station in Chicago, the one who'd given me directions to where I could board The Diamond Line thirty-six hours earlier.

"What is this, some kind of cosmic personal development workshop?" I asked.

"A Cosmic workshop?" the old man said with a laugh. "Well, yes, I guess that's as good a description as any. I've got to remember that one. But you haven't answered my question."

"Which was...?"

"Have you figured out why you're here?" the old man asked again.

"Yes," I said. "And while I don't understand how you made any of this happen, thank you."

"Don't thank me—I didn't do anything," he said. "And why are you acting like we're done here?"

"What?"

"Son, we're just getting started," the wrinkled old man said with a devious smile.

"No!" I said. "I've got to get home to my wife. She's probably worried sick."

"You like to eat, right?" the old man said.

"Eat? What on earth are you talking about?"

"Stay for dinner," the old man said.

"Dinner?" I snapped. "You need to tell me how I get back home. Now!"

The old man stood. "All in good time. For now, shine your shoes and get your suit pressed. And, dear Lord, borrow a tie from Dr. Conwell. The one you own is hideous."

*　　*　　*

I hurried to the main passenger car and found Florence and Dr. Conwell deep in conversation. "Sorry to interrupt," I said.

"We were just discussing Florence's future as an author and lecturer," Dr. Conwell said. "You must admit, Florence gave quite an impressive talk. I believe people were as enthusiastic over her words as they were for mine, and she wasn't even prepared!"

"That is not entirely true," Florence interjected. "I have always felt an opportunity to speak would one day present itself, and when it did I was determined to be prepared."

"So the speech you gave, you had it prepared?"

"Of course I did," Florence said beaming. "Everyone should have a few words prepared in case the need should arise."

"Bravo!" Conwell exclaimed. "You have just proven my belief that when opportunity knocks, one must be prepared to open the door."

I felt a tinge of jealousy at all the attention being paid to Florence. "Well, as much as I'd like to stay and chat, I've got to get ready for our big dinner tonight," I said. "Dr. Conwell, would it be okay if I had some cleaning charges put on your account? I'll pay you back."

"Of course, Christopher," Conwell said.

"Dinner?" Florence asked. "Are Dr. Conwell and I invited?"

I realized I was taking a chance, not knowing what the old wrinkled man had in mind, but spoke up anyway. "Of course you're invited."

"What time should we be ready?" Florence asked.

"Seven o'clock sharp," I said. "And, Dr. Conwell—can I borrow one of your neckties?"

*　*　*

We were sitting in the passenger car, Florence in a long purple gown adorned with white lace and white gloves that went past her elbows, and me in my black wool suit and one of Dr. Conwell's neckties.

"Do you believe in thought manifestation?" Florence asked.

"You mean like having the ability to turn thoughts into things?" I asked.

"Yes! Precisely!" Florence said. "Have you ever witnessed it?"

"I'm not sure," I said.

"I have," Florence said.

"Really?"

"Of course," Florence said. "I witness it virtually every day."

"Give me an example," I said.

"I would think my best example would be you, Christopher," Florence said.

"Me?"

"Yes, *you*," Florence said. "You see, yesterday—as I boarded the train—I created a picture in my mind. And do you know what I pictured?"

I shook my head.

"I pictured you, Christopher," she said. "I manifested you with my thoughts! I believe that is how you ended up here on this train. Do you not see?"

I stayed quiet.

"When I say I manifested *you*, what I mean is that I created the image of meeting *someone* who would help me decide the direction of my future," Florence said. "And then I held that picture in my mind's eye—never letting go of it for a second—with the complete belief that what I wanted would present itself."

"That's pretty weird," I said.

"Are you saying that you do not believe me?" Florence asked.

"No, it's just that I was starting to believe that *I* had manifested *you*," I said with a laugh. "Both you and Dr. Conwell, the train, and everything else."

"Who knows, Christopher, perhaps you have," Florence said. "Perhaps we are all—each and every one of us—manifesting what we want at all times, with the result of our collective being the world that surrounds us."

It sounded crazy, but why not? With everything I'd been through during the last few days, I knew that *anything* was possible.

Dr. Conwell then entered the train car, smartly dressed in a white dinner jacket and black slacks, a black bow tie, and black patent leather shoes. "So when does this dinner of yours begin?" he asked as he approached the two of us.

It was a good question.

I only wished I had an answer.

◇

"People might not get all they work for in this world, but they must certainly work for all they get."

—Frederick Douglass

Track Seventeen:

THE INVITATION THAT WASNT

Dr. Conwell and Florence were getting frustrated, and I didn't blame them in the least. Almost two hours had passed and nothing had happened.

The whole thing was making me crazy.

"This is that old man's fault!" I huffed.

Conwell and Florence exchanged glances as I stepped out on the rear platform of the train to get some air. When I returned five minutes later, I found Dr. Conwell and Florence waiting for me with somber looks on their faces.

"What's wrong?" I asked.

Conwell cleared his throat. "The railway porter just delivered invitations to a formal dinner party being held by my old friend, Phineas Barnum, to be held in his private railcar."

"Phineas?" I asked.

"Phineas Taylor Barnum," Florence said.

It took a moment for me to realize what they were talking about, and then it hit me. "Are you saying we've been invited to have dinner with P.T. Barnum?"

"Not exactly," Florence said.

"It seems there are only two invitations, Christopher," Dr. Conwell said in a subdued tone. "One for myself, and a second invitation for Florence."

"I... I don't understand," I stammered.

"If it is of any consolation," Conwell said, "the only reason we were invited was because P.T. heard Florence and I give our talks earlier."

"That's true, Christopher," Florence said. "I am quite sure I would not have been included had I not agreed to speak."

"Wow!" I said, trying to sound happy for Florence, while secretly seething and trying to hide my anger.

"Dr. Conwell asked if we might be able to bring a friend along," Florence continued, "but apparently there is only room for six seats at the dinner table."

"Six? Who are the other three?" I asked, thinking it was impossible to feel any worse than I already did.

I was wrong.

"The other three guests will be James Bailey, Frederick Douglass and Andrew Carnegie," Conwell said.

I knew instantly who each of them were, of course.

James Bailey was P.T. Barnum's business partner.

Frederick Douglass was an escaped slave-turned-statesman who'd become one of the most important African-Americans of his time.

And Andrew Carnegie was the richest man in the world—at least in this time.

I knew that Dr. Conwell and Florence felt bad for me, but they couldn't possibly have felt as bad as I did. But more than that, I was confused as to why the wrinkled old man told me to get my suit pressed for a dinner party he knew I was not going to be invited to.

◇ James Anthony Bailey ◇
1847-1906

Track Eighteen:

THE GREATEST PARTY ON EARTH

"Thank you for the generous invitation, Mr. Barnum," Florence said. "Your Pullman car is simply stunning!"

"Kind of you to say," Barnum said.

Sharply dressed in a charcoal-gray tailcoat with black satin lapels and a white embroidered waistcoat, P.T. Barnum was every bit the showman Florence expected. "I decorated the interior myself," Barnum said with pride.

Part tasteful Victorian, part 1880's chic, and part outlandish gaudiness, the interior of Barnum's Pullman car was like a carnival on wheels.

The floors were covered in expensive oriental rugs, with furniture made of polished mahogany and rich upholstery. And then there were the unexpected details that had P.T. Barnum written all over them, including a large glass jar containing what appeared to be a severed human arm preserved in formaldehyde, a stuffed alpaca wearing a Mexican sombrero, and a tribal throne from Africa made of lacquered deer antlers.

"I agree with you Miss Scovel," James Bailey called out from the bar as he poured himself a glass of Scotch. "I think it fair to say that P.T.'s railcar rivals some of the best hotel rooms in the world."

Unlike Barnum, James Bailey's appearance was quite understated. The man was clad in a green two-piece wool-tweed suit over a starched white shirt and a black silk necktie.

"Try as I might to rein in P.T.'s spending, he has spared no expense on décor."

"No need to disparage me simply because I refuse to become a tightfisted penny-pincher like you!" Barnum called to his partner.

Russell Conwell stepped forward and offered his hand. "Good to see you, Phineas. Let me say how much Miss Scovel and I appreciate the invitation."

"Yes, Conwell, it's been far too long," Barnum said. "Had it not been for your talk from the rear of the train in Harrisburg, none of us would have even known you were aboard the train."

"Are we to understand you are to publish a new book?" Bailey asked.

"Yes," Conwell said. "It is to be called *Acres of Diamonds*, as will be my lecture from this point forward."

"A much better title," P.T. Barnum said. "What were you calling it?"

"The Ali Hafed Story," Conwell said.

"Yes, simply dreadful," Barnum said. "Speaking of lectures, might I say that was one wonderful talk you gave, Miss Scovel."

"Thank you, Mr. Barnum," Florence said. "Might I ask where our other guests are?"

"Carnegie is being fashionably late, as usual," Bailey said. "And I fear the convention has caused Frederick a bit of fatigue."

"It would be quite an honor to meet Mr. Douglass," Florence said. "I do so hope he'll make an appearance."

"I'm sure he's just taking a well-deserved rest," Barnum said. "He'll show up eventually."

"Speaking of Frederick Douglass, wasn't that the damnedest thing?" James Bailey said. "Imagine, the idea of a black man getting a vote at the Republican Presidential Convention."

"Indeed!" Barnum replied. "First black man ever to do so."

"If ever a man deserved such an honor—black, white or otherwise—it is Frederick Douglass," Conwell said in agreement.

"A toast then to Fredrick Douglass!" James Bailey said, raising his glass of Scotch and then realizing that neither Conwell nor Florence had been offered drinks. "Where ever are my manners? What can I pour for you both?"

"Nothing for me," Conwell said.

"Not another teetotaler," Bailey said.

"I am afraid so," Conwell said. "But do not let my abstinence stop you from imbibing whatever you wish."

"Good man, Conwell!" Barnum bellowed. "I stopped drinking spirits long ago, and am damn glad I did!"

"That is all very well and good, gentlemen, but I would very much like a glass of red wine," Florence said.

"Excellent," James Bailey said. "I just now opened a bottle of 1879 Lafite-Rothschild Cabernet."

"Dear God," Barnum snorted. "Another perfectly operative mind on the road to destruction. You do realize the act of money-making requires a man to have a clear brain and the ability to see that two and two make four? And are you even of age?"

"I should think seventeen to be old enough for a glass of wine," Florence said. "Besides, I have grown up in a home with progressive parents who would think nothing of it. They trust me enough to travel unaccompanied—do you not think they would trust me enough to sip a glass of God's nectar? And regarding the act of money-making, there are many things that affect a *man's* ability to do so, but certainly you have noticed I am a *woman*."

"That will teach you to tangle with Florence," Conwell said.

"Crack wise all you wish, Miss Scovel, but I contend that no man—*or woman*—can move up the ladder of success without a clear mind to give reason to their plans."

"Excuse my business partner, Florence," Bailey said, handing her a long-stemmed crystal glass of red wine.

84

"Phineas is totally convinced one's judgment is warped by an intoxicating drink—a concept I drink to daily."

"There is no need to get into a twist, Mr. Barnum," Florence said, raising her glass and taking a sip. "A social drink is of no harm to any person."

"Ah! You say! Yet how many good opportunities have passed, never to return, while a person sat sipping a *social glass* with a friend?" Barnum asked.

"If this is how you treat your guests, Mr. Barnum, one must wonder how you behave when entertaining your enemies," Florence said. "Perhaps the difference between us is that I know when to set my glass down, while you do not."

"This is the future I've been telling you about, gentlemen," Barnum said.

"Oh? And what future might that be?" Russell Conwell asked.

"The one in which women have taken charge of commerce, and we men are sent off to wash the dishes," Barnum said.

"Joke as you wish, Mr. Barnum, but being a woman in a man's world is far more difficult than you might imagine. It requires that she think like a man, act like a lady, and look like a young girl—all while working like a dog."

The room went quiet enough to hear a pin drop, and then all three men broke into uproarious laughter.

◇

"Your word is your wand. The words you speak create your own destiny."

—Florence Scovel Shinn

Track Nineteen:

ANDREW CARNEGIE

"Have I missed the joke?" Andrew Carnegie said loudly from the doorway of the railcar.

Dressed in a black waistcoat, with his full beard hanging low on his chest and a black bowler hat perched on top of his head, the large man immediately became the center of attention.

"Ah, Andrew!" Barnum said. "Be forewarned, young Florence here is not to be trifled with."

"Dear God, do not tell me you have invited a feminist to dinner?" Carnegie said as he made his way across the railcar to Florence and extended his hand. "Florence, is it?"

"Florence Scovel," Florence replied. "A pleasure to meet you, Mr. Carnegie, and to the degree I am a feminist, it is only because it is required of me to fulfill my destiny."

"And what destiny might that be?" James Bailey asked.

"To teach women that life is a game, one of boomerangs in which our thoughts, deeds, and words return to us sooner or later with astounding accuracy," Florence said.

"Worse than a feminist," Andrew Carnegie snorted. "This young lady is a rabble-rousing new thought spiritualist."

"I should think Florence takes that as a compliment," Conwell said, extending his hand to Carnegie.

"A disciple of yours no doubt, eh, Conwell?" Andrew Carnegie said as he took Conwell's hand and shook it.

"Jesus had disciples, Carnegie," Conwell said. "I merely have friends, and Florence here is a good one indeed."

"Please ignore my bluster, Miss Scovel," Carnegie said. "I have nothing against any woman who wishes to play in the business world, providing she is also well-behaved in the home."

"Well-behaved women rarely make history, Mr. Carnegie," Florence said. "They make dinner."

"I warned you, Carnegie!" Barnum snorted. "If you wish to tangle with Florence, do so at your own risk."

"I mean no disrespect to Miss Scovel," Carnegie said. "But you must understand, my attitude regarding a woman's value comes from years in the rough-and-tumble world of oil derricks and steel mills. And in these endeavors, I suggest, no woman could ever hope to succeed."

Florence smiled before responding. "That is fascinating, Mr. Carnegie. Do tell me, how many women have you hired to test this theory of yours?"

"Very well, I give up!" Carnegie exclaimed.

*   *   *

Ten minutes later, disguised as a tuxedoed waiter, I pushed a service cart into P.T. Barnum's railcar. "Excuse me, where would you like me to place the hors d'oeuvres?"

"In the drawing room, please," Bailey responded.

"While the food is being set, come look at my latest curiosity—a shrunken head that was purchased from a tribesman on the island of Borneo," Barnum said as he rose to his feet.

Having no interest in seeing a shrunken head, Florence went to the drawing room to peruse the magnificent spread of appetizers, including liver pate and toast points, beluga caviar, steamed mussels, jumbo shrimp with cocktail sauce, cracked-wheat crackers, and miniature croissants with assorted jellies and jams.

"This looks magnificent!" Florence said. But when she looked up, her eyes went wide and her mouth fell open. The waiter wasn't just any waiter—it was me.

"Christopher?" Florence whispered. "What on earth are you doing here?"

"What does it look like? I'm serving appetizers," I said.

"I can see that," Florence hissed. "Where did you get that uniform?"

"I highly recommend the shrimp," I said, ignoring her question. "I had three of them on the way over, but stay away from the cocktail sauce—too much horseradish."

"Did you steal it?" Florence asked in a stern voice.

"No, Florence, I did not steal it."

"Then pray tell, how..."

"I traded my cell phone for it," I said with a grin, proud of my resourcefulness. "I mean, the battery is dead. And since the guy won't be able to get a replacement for about a hundred years, I figure the future is safe enough."

Just then, Russell Conwell entered the drawing room and walked over to Florence. "Not interested in shrunken heads, Florence? I admit that I, too, find such things—"

Conwell stopped speaking mid-sentence when he saw me. "Christopher?" he stammered.

"Desperate times require desperate measures," I said.

Florence was not amused. "It seems that Christopher believes the solution to his situation requires engaging in an act of subterfuge."

I wasn't having any of it.

"Listen, I'm supposed to be here!" I said a bit too loudly. "You know how you said that we all manifest the world around us, Florence? Well— if you're right—then I manifested this. And if I manifested it, then there's got to be a reason, right?"

I placed the final plates on the table and closed the cart.

"What is your plan, Christopher?" Conwell asked.

"I'm not sure," I said. "But I'll try to have it figured out by the time I come back with dinner."

◊ Andrew Carnegie ◊

1859-1922

Track Twenty:

THE PURPOSE OF WEALTH

Most people would have considered P.T. Barnum's dinner party an evening of fun and merriment. Florence, on the other hand, considered her time with these amazing men an advanced course in successful living. This being the case, she directed the conversation as quickly as she could toward the topics she was most interested in.

"Since I find myself surrounded by gentlemen of such achievement, I think it a wasted opportunity were I not to inquire as to your personal attitudes on wealth," Florence started.

"Wealth? One need only look around this very instant to know my answer on the subject," P.T. Barnum said. "You gain wealth as quickly as you can, and then ensure every penny of it is spent before they lay you in the grave."

"I am not so sure about the spending aspect, for I am much more keen on giving," Conwell said, "but I do concur when it comes to obtaining wealth. I will go so far as to contend it is not only a blessing to obtain wealth, it is every man's duty to do so."

"Here! Here!" James Bailey said, raising his glass. "To the duty of obtaining wealth."

"And you, Mr. Carnegie?" Florence asked. "As you are the richest man in the world, I imagine you have strong opinions on the matter."

"You flatter me, Miss Scovel, but this very morning the papers gave the title of richest man to Mr. Rothschild," Carnegie said. "The distinction between us, of course, is that every penny of my wealth made its way into my coffers by the sweat of my brow and blisters on my own two hands. Mr. Rothschild, on the other hand, inherited his fortune—an act I consider to be nothing short of stealing."

"Here! Here!" James Bailey proclaimed, raising his glass again. "To hard work and blisters!"

"So it is the act of hard work that makes the man?" Florence asked, an eyebrow raised in skepticism.

"Of course it is," Carnegie snapped. "Do you not agree?"

"Remember the proverb of Solomon?" P.T. Barnum interjected. "He becometh poor that dealeth with slack of hand, but the hand of the diligent maketh rich."

"Solomon was a wise man, one who most certainly engaged in the action of labor," Florence said. "But I have seen too many men with broken backs, years spent laboring behind the plow—or shoveling ore into the furnaces in your sweat shops, Mr. Carnegie—yet I can see no wealth that has come their way from such slavery. I see only the sadness of lives wasted in states of deep misery."

"If Frederick were here, I believe he would concur," Conwell said. "As a slave who pushed a plow and picked cotton in the summer sun, I imagine he would agree the accumulation of wealth is not in direct proportion to the sweat that flows from the brow."

James Bailey raised his glass for another toast, then stopped himself. Toasting slavery seemed rather inappropriate.

"Very well," Carnegie said. "I concede that hard work is not the only way to wealth. As I pointed out, one can always inherit it."

"I am quite certain Florence is thinking there is another key not yet discussed," Conwell said. "Florence?"

"Yes," Florence said, taking her cue. "I believe the key to riches is more of a mental endeavor than a physical one."

"Thinking doesn't move the plow," Carnegie said.

"I contend that, for the greatest number of people, the doors to wealth are locked because they think themselves unworthy of the abundance that is rightfully theirs," Florence said.

"A misguided notion if ever there was one, which I shall chalk up to your youth," Carnegie said.

"Best watch yourself, Carnegie," P.T. Barnum said. "Florence may be young, but dare I say she is beyond her years when it comes to the topic of attaining wealth."

"Ah! We were just speaking of you, Douglass," Barnum said.

Everyone stood as Frederick Douglas—resplendently dressed in a purple velvet waistcoat, white-starched shirt with a stand-up collar, black silk cravat, gray-striped trousers, and black boots—entered the railcar.

"Our man, Douglass, risen from the dead," Bailey said.

"I feared I may have overslept, but I see that is not the case," Frederick Douglass said, taking the only empty chair at the table.

"To the contrary, old chap, your timing seems to be perfect," Barnum said as the door to the Pullman car swung open again and two tuxedoed waiters pushed service carts into the room.

Florence and Dr. Conwell exchanged knowing glances and held their breath.

Sure enough, the second of the two waiters was exactly who they expected.

*   *   *

"We were in the throes of a deep discussion when you arrived," Carnegie said to Frederick Douglass. "Care to join in?"

"May I ask the topic?" Douglass asked.

"I was sharing my belief that the thoughts one holds within the mind are the essential element to acquiring wealth," Florence said.

"Yes, and I was explaining to young Miss Scovel here that dispensing such misguided drivel to an unsuspecting public borders on motivational malpractice," Carnegie admonished.

"I find this topic interesting indeed," Douglass said. "Tell me more of your theory, Miss Scovel."

Florence wasted no time. "It is my belief that every great work, every large accomplishment, has been brought into manifestation by holding onto a vision created in the mind of the achiever."

"I think the young lady may be onto something," Barnum said.

"Please, Phineas, do not encourage the young lass," Carnegie implored.

"Now, I am not saying this simply to prop young Florence up," Barnum insisted. "I say it because I know it to be true. Everything I have ever achieved was indeed created twice—first in my mind, and then in reality."

"I should think the Barnum & Bailey Circus to be a perfect example," James Bailey said. "I remember the day P.T. came to me with the idea for the three rings, and I tell you it was nothing more than that—an idea—a creation within the confines of P.T.'s imagination. Only then did the idea come into existence."

"Exactly my point," Florence said. "I see the visions of man's creations as mental images that provide a framework upon which one begins building."

"Like the drawings of an architect, or the maps of an explorer?" Douglass asked.

"Precisely," Florence said. "It is only after the map becomes firm in one's mind that it can become firm in one's reality."

I moved the service cart around the table, setting china plates before each person and finding myself fascinated by the conversation. I was also starting to get a bit annoyed by Andrew Carnegie's rudeness toward Florence, which, at certain moments, bordered on bullying.

"A man must do more than *wish* for wealth; he must take decisive action," Carnegie said.

"I said nothing of wishing," said Florence defiantly. "I am suggesting that if one wants abundance to arrive, they must *expect it* as if the abundance was theirs already. Each person has the right to the abundance that is theirs for the claiming, but erroneous beliefs block the arrival of this wealth in the external world."

"Pure humbug!" Carnegie snorted.

"Not so quickly, Carnegie," Russell Conwell said, coming to Florence's rescue. "On this matter, I completely concur."

"Certainly you are joking, Conwell," Carnegie said. "I know you are a man of God, but I would never have taken you for some sort of frou-frou spiritualist."

"Allow me to share a story, and since dinner is upon us, I shall keep it brief," Conwell said. "One evening, at one of my lectures, a young man told me any person with money must be dishonest. I responded by telling him the reason he had no money was because the foundation of his beliefs were altogether false—that men like Carnegie here—were by and large honest men who came by their wealth through hard work and discipline. And do you know what this young man said?"

"I can only imagine," Carnegie said.

"He said he hated the likes of the Carnegies and the Rockefellers so greatly that he was thankful to God for having made him poor! Well, I do not wish to see more of that kind of God's poor on the streets, not when that man could have been rich just as easily."

"This man of whom you speak," Carnegie said. "His opinions of me are of no interest, as they have no impact on my ability to accumulate wealth."

"You are missing the point entirely, Mr. Carnegie," Florence said. "The young man's opinions of you are not the locks on the door to your wealth—they are the locks on the door to *his* abundance."

"Well, good, I say!" Carnegie bellowed. "The less this man has, the more that can be accumulated by me."

"My heart weeps for you, Carnegie," Fredrick Douglass said. "Have you not yet discovered that it is the act of giving that opens the way for receiving? I pray for your last act on this Earth to be one of giving."

"And I pray my last act on this Earth will be the accumulation of another dollar," Carnegie said. "One which I intend to take to the grave with me."

That was when I lost it.

◇

"A man who acquires the ability to take full possession of his own mind may take possession of anything else to which he is justly entitled."

–Andrew Carnegie

MY SEAT AT THE TABLE

Andrew Carnegie's bullying attacks on Florence had finally driven me to the point where I found it impossible to stay silent a minute longer.

"Then why did you give it all away?" I said loudly enough that every head at the table turned and looked in my direction.

"Are you addressing me?" Andrew Carnegie asked.

Florence shot me a wild look.

"If I might—" Dr. Conwell began.

"Thanks, Dr. Conwell, but I've got this," I said, cutting him off. I took a deep breath, turned to Andrew Carnegie, and continued. "Yes, Mr. Carnegie, I am addressing you. What you just said about your last act on Earth being to make another dollar and take it to the grave with you? Well, that's not what you end up doing."

"Conwell, is this a prank of your doing?" Carnegie snapped. "Or you, Barnum?"

Barnum shrugged and remained silent.

"Christopher, please allow me to explain," Conwell said.

"If you know this man, Conwell, then explain—"

"My name is Christopher Powers, and Dr. Conwell has nothing to do with this," I said, taking off the white tuxedo and bow tie. "I don't expect you to believe a word of what I'm about to tell you, but it has to do with your money."

"My money? What could a waiter possibly know—?"

"I'm not a waiter, Mr. Carnegie," I said interrupting, "and I know a great deal about your money, starting with the assertion that you're going to take it all with you—it's just not true. The millions you've spent so much of your life hoarding, well—you change your mind and you give it all away—to libraries and colleges and to fund the Carnegie Mellon University and Carnegie Hall."

Andrew Carnegie shot to his feet. "This carnival act of yours, young man, I am not amused with it at all. And the institutions of which you speak do not even exist."

"They will," I said.

"You better listen to him, Andrew," Conwell said.

"Yes, you must believe him!" Florence said jumping in.

"I am not saying any of this to amuse you, sir," I said in as calm a tone as possible, though my heart was pounding out of my chest. "I'm telling you this to let you know that what Mr. Douglass said earlier is true—the act of giving is the thing that opens the way for receiving—and you will eventually see it's true and find more joy giving your money away than you ever did earning it."

Carnegie stormed to the Pullman car door. "I will endure this no longer!" Then he slammed the door hard behind him. Other than the sound of my rapid breathing, it was so quiet you could have heard a proverbial pin drop.

"What did you say your name was?" P.T. Barnum asked.

"This is my friend, Christopher Powers," Russell Conwell said, patting me on the back. "He is the young man who provided me with the title for my Acres of Diamonds talk."

"What's more, Christopher is from the future," Florence said in a hushed tone.

"I do not understand how he knows such things," James Bailey said, "but whether this young man is from the future or not, we have just witnessed an enormously brave display of heart. Dear Lord, the number of times I wanted to give Carnegie a taste of his own medicine." Bailey raised his glass and said, "To Christopher! A man of courage!"

"I am an equal believer that fortune favors the brave," Frederick Douglass said, raising his glass, with Dr. Conwell, Florence and P.T. Barnum doing the same.

"If I am not mistaken, Phineas, it appears as if a seat at the table has just come available," Conwell said.

"Indeed it has," P.T. Barnum said. "Christopher, I do not suppose you would care to join us?"

◇

"All human beings can alter their lives by altering their attitudes. Do your duty, and a little more, and the future will take care of itself."

—Andrew Carnegie

Track Twenty-Two:

VOICES OF THE DEAD

The next two hours in P.T. Barnum's railcar was a non-stop barrage of questions about the future.

"What you have shared is beyond belief," P.T. Barnum said, "yet I have no doubt that you have spoken the truth."

"Were it not for Conwell's endorsement of the lad, I am unsure if I would give these fantastical claims any credence," James Bailey said. "Quite amazing and yet disconcerting."

"Yes, that is the word I have been searching for," Frederick Douglass said. "Very disconcerting. I feel that if God intended for us to know of these events, He would speak his plans to us directly."

"In any case," Russell Conwell said, "we must each remember our pledge to go to the grave without sharing a word of what has been said here to another living soul."

"I agree," P.T. Barnum said. "What we have been privy to must go no further than this train."

"Agreed," Bailey said, raising his glass once again.

"You have my word on it," Florence said. "Yet, it is my belief that we have all been changed through the knowing of these things, whether we speak of them or not."

A sense of relief washed over me as, one by one, each person nodded their heads in agreement. At the same time, I feared Florence might well have been right. Telling them about the future may have been the ringing of a bell that could never be un-rung.

* * *

After dessert had been served by the other waiter, a photographer arrived with a large antique box-camera on a tripod—at least the camera was an antique to me.

"Ah, Eakins!" James Bailey exclaimed as the photographer entered the railcar. "Everyone, this is Thomas Eakins. He does the most marvelous photographs, and I have engaged him to make one of us all."

"Too bad for Carnegie," P.T. Barnum said with a laugh.

"True enough, but his loss is our gain," James Bailey said, waving me over to join the group.

"No, that's okay," I said. After all, I wasn't even supposed to be there.

"Nonsense," Bailey said. "You took Andrew's seat at the table and, by God, you shall take his spot in this photographic image."

We lined up, the six of us—Dr. Conwell on the far left, followed by Frederick Douglass, myself, Florence, P.T. Barnum, and James Bailey on the far right—each of us holding our facial expressions as still as possible. I was so excited to have been included, I made the mistake of smiling broadly, forced to hold the pose the entire time.

It took Thomas Eakins fifteen minutes to complete the elaborate photographic process, which involved large silver plates and light-sensitive silver iodide. The experience made me appreciate the many inventions of the last century even more.

"I know it's getting late," I said once Thomas Eakins had gone, "but if you don't mind, I have a few questions of my own."

"Questions for us?" P.T. Barnum asked. "What could we possibly know that would not become antiquated before the day you were born?"

"Not about events," I said. "My questions are about beliefs—the beliefs and behaviors you have used to achieve your success, which I would think are pretty much timeless."

"Very well, then," P.T. Barnum said. "Let me begin by admitting that—like Carnegie—it has always been my aim to put money in my coffers. However, unlike Andrew, I have suffered many economic reversals. And even under the weight of crushing failure and massive debt, I have always found means to remain happy and grateful."

"I can attest to that," Bailey said. "P.T. believes the noblest art is that of making others happy."

Barnum smiled, appreciative of the compliment. "Promoting one's wares is a simple process comprised of two steps; the first is to find out what the other person wants, and the second is to provide it to them."

"I fear you are being too modest, Phineas," Russell Conwell said. "Do not forget that young Christopher here is seeking the truth about your success, and you have minimized your true strengths."

"Yes, Mr. Barnum, please expand upon your thoughts," Florence said.

"Very well," Barnum said. "I shall add that one must be constantly willing to blow one's own horn, for at the core of every successful endeavor is the act of promotion. And make no mistake—without promotion, something terrible happens... and that something is nothing."

"Your success is beyond remarkable, Mr. Barnum," Florence said after the laughter died away, "but I do have a bone to pick with you."

Barnum arched his eyebrows. "And what bone might that be, Miss Scovel?"

"It is in regards to your belief that all spiritualists are frauds," Florence said.

"Ah! I should well have known you would attack me there," Barnum said with a laugh. "Don't get me wrong, Miss Scovel, I have no quarrel with entertainers who use hype and humbug to promote themselves, but I have nothing but contempt for so-called spiritual mediums who claim the ability to hear the voices of the dead. To me, such people are charlatans who deserve to be jailed, not hailed."

"Yes, I have heard of your standing offer to pay $500 to anyone providing proof of the ability to do so," Florence said. "And this offer, does it still stand?"

"Indeed it does," P.T. Barnum said.

"Very well then," Florence said as she rose to her feet, crossed the railcar and pulled a book from the shelf. "Allow me to read a passage from *Voltaire's Candide,*" Florence said before beginning to read an excerpt:

> *There was never anything so gallant, so spruce, so brilliant, and so well disposed as the two armies. Trumpets, fifes, hautboys, drums, and cannon made music such as Hell itself had never heard. The cannons first of all laid flat about six thousand men on each side; the muskets swept away from this best of worlds nine or ten thousand ruffians who infested its surface. The bayonet was also a sufficient reason for the death of several thousands. The whole might amount to thirty thousand souls. Candide, who trembled like a philosopher, hid himself as well as he could during this heroic butchery.*

Florence closed the book. "If I am not mistaken, Voltaire is quite gone from this Earth, is he not Mr. Barnum?"

"He is indeed," Barnum conceded.

"And would you concur, Mr. Barnum, that we have just heard his words from beyond the grave?" Florence asked.

"Look like she has you, old boy!" James Bailey said with a touch of glee in his voice.

P.T. Barnum stood and pulled a roll of bills from his pocket. "I shall pay you your due for your cleverness, Ms. Scovel, on one condition."

"And that condition being...?

"That you promise to tell no one of this loophole in my offer," P.T. Barnum said.

"Thank you, Mr. Barnum," Florence said. "But before you return your billfold, I believe you also owe $500 to our friend Christopher."

"To Christopher? For what do I owe him?" P.T. Barnum barked. "He has demonstrated no such clever trick."

"To the contrary," Florence said. "Allow me to do the demonstration, this time with cleverness involved." Florence turned to where I was sitting. "Christopher, can you hear my voice?"

"Yes, Florence, I hear you."

"And what about the others in this room? Have you been able to hear them as well?"

"Yes, I have," I said, suddenly realizing where Florence was going.

Florence turned back to P.T. Barnum. "May I contend that each of us in this railcar shall have left this Earthly plane long before Christopher is born, yet he has heard our voices clearly. In that way, Mr. Barnum, to Christopher we are all quite dead."

"I hope you have deep pockets, P.T.," Conwell said. "It seems that Florence has bested you again."

◇ Frederick Douglass ◇
1818-1895

◇

"If you wish to be great, you must begin where you are, and what you are."

–Russell H. Conwell

Track Twenty-Three:

P.T. BARNUM'S CHALLENGE

"In the spirit of equal play, I have a bone to pick with you as well, Miss Scovel," P.T. Barnum said.

"Do tell," Florence said.

"Regarding your belief that one can turn mental visions into real things," Barnum said. "Is it your position that this can be achieved for anything one wants, large or small?"

"Most certainly," Florence said. "If one wishes a thing badly enough and can hold the vision of it in the mind's eye long enough, it must—by universal law—manifest in the real world."

Barnum nodded as if in agreement, then continued. "And is it your belief that this process can be used for any quantity of things one wishes without limit?"

"I feel as if you are examining me during a trial," Florence said.

"To the contrary, Miss Scovel—I am not examining you; I am examining your theory," Barnum said. "So, please answer."

"Yes, the process works for any one thing and for any number of things," Florence said.

"This is where I believe you have it wrong," Barnum said. "While I am on board with the general concept, I believe the reason many persons are kept poor is because they are *too visionary*. Every project looks to them like certain success, and, therefore, they keep changing from one business to another, always in hot water, always under the harrow.

"Clouding one's mind with visions of this and that—of more and more and even more after that—is the folly of fools! I contend that many a man has acquired a fortune by doing one thing thoroughly, while his neighbor remains poor for life because he has 'half done' many.

"Were I to be asked for the single key to success, most would assume my answer would be the art of showmanship or the power of promotion, but it is not," Barnum said. "My answer would be contained in a single word…"

Ever the showman, P.T. Barnum paused for several seconds before delivering the answer, and I found myself on the edge of my seat.

"*Focus,*" Barnum said finally. "That is the bone I must pick with your theory, Miss Scovel. In my experience, successful men do not scatter their powers—they focus on one thing and do that thing with boldness! They engage in one kind of business only, and stick to it faithfully until they have succeeded, knowing the constant hammering of a single nail will drive it home at last. When a man's undivided attention is centered on one object—*and one object alone*—the mind will constantly be suggesting improvements of value that would escape him if a dozen different subjects occupied his brain at once. Many a fortune has slipped through a man's fingers because he was engaged in too many occupations at a time."

"As one who agrees wholeheartedly with your beliefs, I must say that P.T. has made a good case, Florence," Dr. Conwell said.

"I agree," James Bailey chimed in. "There is good sense in the old caution against having too many irons in the fire."

The group went silent and waited as Florence considered her response. Finally she spoke. "Since my earliest years, I have been possessed by two dreams; one to become an artist, and the other to be an author and lecturer like Dr. Conwell. And though I believe a person can manifest anything they wish, personal experience suggests one cannot manifest everything they wish all at once and that holding two goals in one mind at the same time may indeed be one goal too many."

Florence opened her purse and withdrew the $500 she had won from P.T. Barnum minutes earlier. "I believe this belongs to you again, Mr. Barnum."

Barnum shook his head. "I prefer to invest those funds in you, Florence, for you are the rarest of birds. I have no doubt that one day in the future—long after we have all passed and lay still in our graves—your words will be heard by millions, and they shall help change the world."

"Do you really believe that, Mr. Barnum?" Florence asked.

"Most certainly!" Barnum said, turning to his business partner. "James, lead us in one last toast."

"Yes, why not?" Bailey said, raising his glass. "Here's to the crazy ones. The misfits. The rebels. To the round pegs in the square holes. The ones who see things differently!"

Wait a second, I thought...

Just then, Andrew Carnegie appeared in the railcar doorway. "To those who are not fond of rules, who have no respect for the status quo. You can quote them, disagree with them, glorify them or vilify them..."

I know this...

"...about the only thing you can't do is ignore them," Frederick Douglass said chiming in. "Because they change things. They push the human race forward. And while some may see them as the crazy ones, we see genius..."

That's when I realized everyone was reciting the words from that famous Apple TV commercial, the one they did for the Super Bowl in 1984.

"It's two in the morning, Christopher," Conwell said. "Come to bed."

But it wasn't Conwell's voice coming from his mouth—it was Katie's.

I opened my eyes and found myself on the sofa, the living room dark except for the TV, and Katie standing over me.

"It's two in the morning, Christopher," Katie said again. "Come to bed."

Then I noticed the television was still on, the Steve Jobs biography just ending.

"The people who are crazy enough to think they can change the world," Steve Jobs said, "are the ones who do."

I reached over and turned off the TV.

And then—sitting in the darkness but awake now, I knew...

Katie hadn't suggested I take the train after all.

There had been no ticket on The Diamond Line.

No speeches in Cleveland or Harrisburg from the rear platform of the train.

No Frederick Douglass, no Florence Scovel, no dinner party in P.T. Barnum's Pullman car.

None of it was real.

It had all been a dream.

Track Twenty-Four:

LETTING GO OF THE DREAM

I did not blame Katie for not believing me.

After all, who in their right mind would believe that I'd spent three days on a train in the year 1888 with Russell Conwell, P.T. Barnum, James Bailey, Andrew Carnegie, Frederick Douglass and Florence Scovel?

And the more I pushed, the more I tried to get Katie to understand—to believe that what I'd experienced was real—the crazier I sounded. So I decided the best course of action was to simply let it go.

Well, almost.

There was no way to let go of the lessons I'd learned on The Diamond Line... *real or not.*

There was no way of forgetting the perspectives I'd learned from the legends I'd met... *real or not.*

There was no way of releasing the feeling I had actually traveled back to 1888... *real or not.*

More than anything, there was no ignoring the obvious truth of the main lesson I'd learned—that every resource required to be successful was within my grasp—here and now—right where I was.

I had found my acres of diamonds.

*   *   *

The second day after the dream, I went to the computer and—one by one—I pulled up the Wikipedia pages for each of the people I'd met during the dream, beginning with Russell Conwell:

114

Russell Conwell
February 15, 1843 – December 6, 1925

Born in South Worthington, Massachusetts, Conwell was a well-known Baptist minister, lecturer and philanthropist. He is best known as the founder and first president of Temple University in Philadelphia, Pennsylvania, and for his inspirational lecture, Acres of Diamonds.

Acres of Diamonds originated as a speech that Conwell delivered over 6,000 times around the world. A book by the same title was first published in 1890 by the John Y. Huber Company of Philadelphia. Temple University was built from the income earned from this book and speech.

Then I moved on to the others...

Phineas Taylor (P.T.) Barnum
July 5, 1810 – April 7, 1891

Born in Bethel, Connecticut, P.T. Barnum embarked on an entertainment career at a very early age, becoming a famous author, publisher, politician and philanthropist. But he will forever be remembered most for founding the Barnum & Bailey Circus with business partner James Bailey. Barnum suffered a stroke in 1890 during a performance. Prior to his death, Barnum gave permission to the Evening Sun *newspaper to print his obituary because he wanted to read of his own death.*

James Anthony Bailey
July 4, 1847 – April 11, 1906

An American circus ringmaster who, together with showman P.T. Barnum, established the Barnum and Bailey's Circus (for which Bailey was instrumental in obtaining Jumbo the Elephant) in 1881. Upon P.T. Barnum's death in 1891, Bailey purchased the circus from Barnum's widow. Bailey continued touring the eastern United States until he took his circus to Europe. The circus was sold to the Ringling Brothers in 1907, a year after Bailey's death.

Frederick Douglass
February 1818 – February 20, 1895

A social reformer, lecturer, statesman, abolitionist, early supporter of women's suffrage, and author of several autobiographies in which he eloquently described his experiences as a slave, including Life and Times of Frederick Douglass, *published in 1881 and revised in 1892. At the age of 12, the wife of a slave owner taught Douglass the alphabet, though illegal and against her husband's wishes. Douglass would later be quoted as saying, "Once you learn to read, you will be forever free."*

Andrew Carnegie
November 25, 1835 – August 11, 1919

A Scottish-American industrialist who led the expansion of the American steel industry in the late 19th century, Carnegie became one of the highest profile philanthropists of his time. In an article titled "The Gospel of Wealth" (published in 1889 after a near death experience in a train accident a year earlier), Carnegie called on the rich to use their wealth to improve society, setting off a wave of philanthropy unlike anything seen before.

Florence Scovel Shinn
September 24, 1871 – October 17, 1940

Born in New Jersey and educated in Philadelphia, Florence Scovel Shinn was an American artist who became one of America's New Thought spiritual teachers and metaphysical writers of her time. She is best known for her books, The Game of Life and How to Play It, *(1925) and* The Secret Door to Success, *(1940). Scovel was quoted as saying, "The invisible forces are ever working for man who is always 'pulling the strings' himself, though he does not know it.*

Owing to the vibratory power of words, whatever man voices, he begins to attract." Motivational author Louise Hay acknowledges Florence Scovel Shinn as an early influence.

I know it sounded strange, but I missed them all already. At least there were plenty of books and reading materials available to me—entire library shelves worth—so I could visit them anytime I wished.

But there was one thing that really bothered me.

It was Florence's biography.

I'd known who each of the others were before the dream. They were famous. I'd read things by them and about them. I'd studied them in school and had seen biographies about them on TV.

But Florence?

I was 100 percent certain I had never heard the name Florence Scovel before the night of the dream.

Yet every single thing in her internet bio fit exactly with what I'd experienced, what I knew about her as a young woman with limitless goals and dreams.

Right down to her age.

Her biography said she was born in September 1871. In my dream, it was 1888.

Seventeen.

In any case, even if it had been a dream, the Florence I'd met on the train had done everything she said she wanted to do. Seventeen-year-old Florence Scovel had turned her thoughts into reality and manifested the life of her dreams.

Imagine that.

EPILOGUE
ONE YEAR LATER...

The final workshop at the IGSBE had just concluded, and Katie and I were trying to get everything we'd accumulated over the three days into our bags.

"You were right," Katie said. "The conference was amazing."

"You were right, too," I said.

"About what?"

"About not coming here last year," I said. "It was too early to come then. And if I had come, I don't think I would have made the most of it."

Which was entirely true because it wasn't until after the dream that I began working the business the way I should have from the very start. Attending IGSBE now—having built a solid business over the last year, right where I was and with the resources I had within my reach—made going to the conference an added bonus, not a Hail Mary.

"Come on," Katie said, glancing at her watch, "we're going to miss our train."

No, it wasn't the Diamond Line—there was no Diamond Line, I knew that now. We'd taken the standard Amtrak service from Chicago to New York, which was a great idea.

Katie's idea.

It was also Katie's to spend a full day on the way back in Philadelphia to see the Liberty Bell, and—of course—to visit Temple University.

* * *

Katie and I were finishing our tour of Temple University, the final stop being the school library.

As we climbed the concrete stairs to the library doors, Katie stopped me. "Chris, look."

It was a banner that read: *Acres of Diamonds, 125th Anniversary, 1890-2015.*

Once inside, we discovered there was a tribute to Dr. Russell Conwell, an entire area with copies of all the books he'd written, historical photographs, and miscellaneous memorabilia from a century earlier.

And there it was.

A photograph, right in the middle of the display. No, I take that back. It was not *a* photograph...

It was *the* photograph.

A wide, black and white glossy print—the edges worn and yellowed with age—with the six of us standing in a line, holding our faces perfectly still for the camera.

"Katie" was all I could manage to say, still trying to wrap my brain around what I was seeing.

"What?" Katie said.

"The photo," I said.

(From left to right): Dr. Russell Conwell, Frederick Douglass, Unidentified Passenger, Florence Scovel-Shinn, P.T. Barnum and James A. Bailey. (From the Phineas Taylor Barnum collection, taken aboard The Diamond Railroad Line, circa 1888. Photograph Credit: Thomas Eakins.)

"How is this possible?" Katie asked.

"I don't know."

"I'm sorry I didn't believe you," Katie said. "It's just that—"

"You don't have to apologize," I said. "I'd almost stopped believing it was real myself."

But now I knew.

The entire thing had *not* been my imagination.

It *had* happened.

I had been there with the rest of them...

On the Diamond Line.

SIX KEY LESSONS FROM
THE DIAMOND LINE

-1-

Everything you need to succeed can be found where you are now.

-2-

It is your duty to become rich.

-3-

Focus on one thing at a time, and do it with boldness.

-4-

Success is a science anyone can master.

-5-

Do not wish for abundance—*expect it.*

-6-

What you think about most must eventually manifest itself in reality.

◇

About The Diamond Line...

The Diamond Line is a fictional story about a real person–Dr. Russell H. Conwell–author of a very real book, *Acres of Diamonds,* one of the most motivational books ever penned.

Additionally, Dr. Conwell delivered his Acres of Diamonds speech over 6,000 times, with a vinyl recording released in 1916, followed by a live radio broadcast in 1923.

While we attempted to stay true to Conwell's original *Acres of Diamonds* story, *The Diamond Line* is ultimately a work of fiction. As such, we allowed ourselves significant creative license. For example, there is no historical record that Russell Conwell ever met a time traveler on a train. But, beyond little things like that, the majority of the dates, locations, inventions, etc., are as accurate and real as possible.

About the Authors...

Richard Fenton & Andrea Waltz are the founders of *Courage Crafters, Inc.*, and have made it their mission to help people reprogram the way they feel about failure, rejection and hearing the word "NO!"

As internationally recognized keynote speakers, Richard Fenton & Andrea Waltz have spoken to some of the largest and most successful organizations in the world, including The Pampered Chef, American Express, Primerica, Utility Warehouse Ltd., Aloette, Samsonite, RE/Max, Kleeneze, Tommy Hilfiger, and many others.

They are the authors of the bestselling book *Go for No!®, The Fear Factory* and *Million Dollar Year.*

For information on *Go for No!®* or about having Richard Fenton & Andrea Waltz speak to your group, visit their website:

www.GoForNo.com

Made in the USA
Charleston, SC
07 November 2015